1000 things you should know about

ancient egypt

Jeremy Smith

MILES KELLY

PUBLISHING

This material was first published as hardback in 2006

This edition published in 2006 by Miles Kelly Publishing Ltd
Bardfield Centre, Great Bardfield, Essex, CM7 4SL

2 4 6 8 10 9 7 5 3 1

Editorial Director: Belinda Gallagher
Art Director: Jo Brewer
Editor: Rosalind McGuire
Volume Designer: Ian Paulyn
Additional Design: Candice Bekir
Image Department Manager: Liberty Newton
Picture Researcher: Laura Faulder
Reprographics: Anthony Cambray, Mike Coupe,
Stephan Davis, Ian Paulyn

British Library Cataloguing-in-Publication Data
A catalogue record for this book is available from the British Library

ISBN 1-84236-710-2

Printed in China

info@mileskelly.net
www.mileskelly.net

All artworks are from the MKP Archives

The publishers would like to thank the following picture sources
whose photographs appear in this book:
Page 59 Guy_Levy/epa/CORBIS
Page 60 Supreme Council Of Antiquities/epa/CORBIS

All photographs from:
Castrol, CMCD, Corbis, Corel, digitalSTOCK, digitalvision, Flat Earth,
Hemera, ILN, John Foxx, PhotoAlto, PhotoDisc, PhotoEssentials,
PhotoPro, Stockbyte

CONTENTS

GROWTH OF AN EMPIRE
6—13

KINGS AND QUEENS
13—24

DAILY LIFE
24—37

RELIGION AND THE AFTERLIFE
38—45

SPORT AND CULTURE
46—55

EXCAVATING THE PAST
55—61

INDEX
62

Who were the Egyptians?

- **Egypt lies** in the north-east of Africa. The river Nile flows through the country and into the Mediterranean Sea through the Delta.

- **People have lived in the area** since the Stone Age, and modern humans arrived about 60,000 years ago.

- **Around 8000 BC**, Northern Africa became arid, but the Nile River Valley remained abundant in food and water.

- **The Khartoum people** arrived in Egypt around 6000 BC. They were the first to domesticate cattle and grow crops in the Nile Valley.

- **The first settlers in ancient Egypt** probably migrated from Palestine, Syria and other parts of Africa.

- **These settlers** were joined 2000 years later by people from the area that is now south Iraq.

- **The period of time** from the founding of these settlements until the unification of Upper and Lower Egypt is known as the Pre-Dynastic era.

- **Historians are not sure** how the end of the Pre-Dynastic era came about.

- **The end of the Pre-Dynastic era** was probably caused by internal factors that brought about a unification of Egypt.

◀ The waters of the river Nile made the civilization of ancient Egypt possible.

On the banks of the Nile

- **Over 90 percent of Egypt** is scorching desert, so it is sometimes called the 'red land'.

- **The Nile is the longest river** in the world – over 6400 km in length. It flows from the highlands of Central Africa to the Mediterranean Sea.

- **The Nile results from three great rivers** coming together – the White Nile, the Atbara and the Blue Nile.

- **Flood season** in Egypt lasts from mid July to the end of September. When the floodwater retreats (between November and March) farmers sow their crops.

- **The first Egyptian farmers** waited for the Nile to flood to nourish their crops, but by 5000 BC they had started to devise ways to control the great river. They dug canals to channel the floodwater to distant fields.

◀ Water was lifted from the Nile using a device called a shaduf.

- **The first reservoir** was built at Fayum, about 60 km southwest of Cairo.

- **Most Egyptians** lived on the banks of the river Nile.

- **The farming year** began when the Nile flooded, washing mineral-rich silt deposits onto the land.

- **The height of the Nile flood** was monitered using 'nilometers' – stone staircases that led down into the river. The speed at which the water covered the steps indicated how fast the flood was likely to be.

- **Even when the floods receded**, the Nile provided the people of Egypt with a life-saving source of water in the otherwise hot and arid landscape.

Lower Egypt

- **Lower Egypt** occupied the northern part of the country, where the Nile divides into the Delta that flows into the Mediterranean Sea.

- **The Nile Delta** dominated Lower Egypt, where the land was fertile and marshy. Lower Egypt had a milder temperature than Upper Egypt, and it also had more rain.

- **Archaeologists do not know** as much about the Pre-Dynastic history of Lower Egypt as they do about Upper Egypt. It is usually divided into five periods by historians.

- **The time before** written history in Egypt is divided into five periods by archaeologists. Each period is named after a site from which tools, pottery and other objects have been excavated.

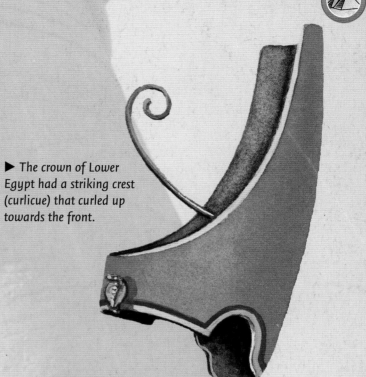

▶ The crown of Lower Egypt had a striking crest (curlicue) that curled up towards the front.

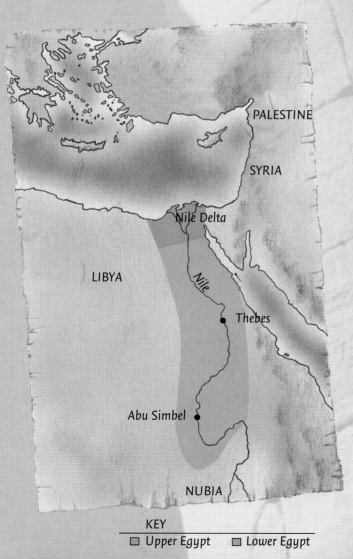

- **Lower Egypt** was known as To-Mehu at the time of the pharaohs. It was divided into 20 areas called 'nomes'.

- **The king of Lower Egypt** wore a red crown, or 'deshret'. It was tall and had a dramatic looking curlicue.

- **Lower Egypt** was represented by the goddess Wadjyt. Usually shown as a cobra, she could also appear as a lion-headed woman or even as a mongoose!

- **Lower Egypt** was heavily influenced by Palestine and Syria. Pottery from these areas, as well as artefacts from Sumeria (lower Euphrates) have been found in the Delta.

- **By the late 4th millennium** BC, the culture of Lower Egypt began to be replaced by that of Upper Egypt. Excavations at Tell el-Farain show that by this time, locally made pottery pieces were being substituted for Upper Egyptian wares.

◀ Lower Egypt was situated at the top of the country in the Nile Delta.

Map labels: PALESTINE, SYRIA, Nile Delta, LIBYA, Nile, Thebes, Abu Simbel, NUBIA

KEY
☐ Upper Egypt   ☐ Lower Egypt

★ STAR FACT ★
The papyrus plant used to flourish in the Delta region. It was used to make paper, and also bound together to make boats, huts and even temples.

Upper Egypt

● **Upper Egypt** is 1250 km in length, stretching south from the Libyan Desert to just past Abu Simbel. The Nile runs through the valley.

● **Historians divide** Pre-Dynastic Upper Egyptian history into three periods – the Badarian (5500–4000 BC), Amratian (4000–3500 BC) and Gerzean (3500–3100 BC).

● **A greater number of ancient sites** have survived in the more favourable archaeological conditions of Upper Egypt.

● **Upper Egypt** was influenced by the culture of the people from the Gerzean Period (3500–3100 BC). Based near Thebes, they moved to Upper Egypt as traders.

● **Upper Egypt** was known as Shemau. The region was divided into 22 nomes.

● **The population of Upper Egypt** was concentrated around a city called Hierakonpolis ('City of the Hawk'). It is likely that this city was ruled by a number of kings.

◄ *The white crown (hedjet) was always associated with Upper Egypt.*

● **The king of Upper Egypt** wore a white crown, or 'hedjet'. It is also referred to as the 'nefer'.

● **The symbol of Upper Egypt** was the lotus flower, or water lily.

● **An important archaeological find** from the region is the knife of Gebel el-Arak. It belonged to a pharaoh of Upper Egypt who lived around 3500 BC. It is decorated with the symbols of the fertility god, Min.

● **The last of the kings** to rule Upper Egypt was called Narmer. His greatest achievement was conquering Lower Egypt and unifying Egypt. This victory was the start of the great age of the pharaohs.

Uniting the kingdoms

● **The union of Upper and Lower Egypt** was very important to the ancient Egyptians. The capital of the new kingdom, Memphis, was close to where the Nile Valley meets the Delta.

● **The ancient Egyptians** divided their kings into families that are now known as dynasties. The 1st Dynasty began when the first king ruled over the united kingdom.

● **Records from** the 1st and 2nd Dynasties are confused. Historians are unable to give names or dates accurately to these rulers.

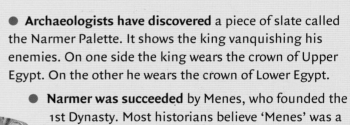

► *The Narmer Palette was found by the British archaeologist J E Quibell in 1898.*

● **Archaeologists have discovered** a piece of slate called the Narmer Palette. It shows the king vanquishing his enemies. On one side the king wears the crown of Upper Egypt. On the other he wears the crown of Lower Egypt.

● **Narmer was succeeded** by Menes, who founded the 1st Dynasty. Most historians believe 'Menes' was a title, and that the king's name was Horus Aha.

● **King Menes** was the founder of the city of Memphis. He also built a great temple there.

● **This period in Egyptian history** saw two dynasties. The first lasted from 2925–2715 BC, and the second lasted from 2715–2658 BC.

● **The kings of the first two dynasties** of the united Egypt all came from a place called This, likely to have been near Abydos in Upper Egypt.

● **The king of the united kingdoms** was usually depicted wearing a double crown, which was made up of the Red Crown of the Delta and the White Crown of the Valley.

The Old Kingdom

● **The Old Kingdom** lasted from 2686–2181 BC and is viewed as one of the more stable times in ancient Egyptian history.

● **During this period,** Egypt used the vast mineral wealth that lay beneath its deserts, and gained wealth through trade.

● **The rulers of this period** left behind a programme of building unprecedented in its scope and imagination.

● **A series of mud-brick temples** were built in the Old Kingdom. They were adorned by statues of gods alongside statues of the kings of Egypt.

● **Under the orders of King Djoser,** a step pyramid was built during the 3rd Dynasty. During the 4th Dynasty straight-sided pyramids were built.

● **At the end of the 4th Dynasty,** a new line of kings took to the throne, calling themselves 'Sons of Ra'.

▶ *The only step pyramid ever completed is situated at Saqqara.*

● **Smaller pyramids were built** during the 5th Dynasty. At Saqqara, they were inscribed with texts to help the dead king reach heaven.

● **Old Kingdom officials** had grand tombs built to mark their deaths.

● **The 6th Dynasty ended** with the death of Queen Nitiqret.

The First Intermediate Period

● **After the stability** and growth of the Old Kingdom, the First Intermediate Period (7th–11th Dynasties) saw the power of the central government in ancient Egypt decline. It began with the death of Queen Nitiqret and lasted until the rule of Mentuhotep II.

● **During this period,** the 7th and 8th Dynasties (2150–2130 BC) were still based at the capital of the united Egypt, Memphis. However, their leaders had great trouble controlling their unruly subjects.

● **The weakness of these rulers** is illustrated by their tombs. They are tiny when compared with the gigantic royal pyramids of the Old Kingdom.

● **The weakness of the ruling kings** at Memphis meant that much of the power was held not by the king but by governors of the different nomes.

● **The rulers of the 9th and 10th Dynasties** established themselves at Herakleopolis, to the south of Memphis. They included Neferkare VII, Kheti and Merikave.

● **After the disintegration** of the Old Kingdom, the governors of Thebes became independent local rulers. Their power soon rivalled that of the 9th and 10th Dynasties at Herakleopolis.

● **One 11th Dynasty ruler** at Thebes was Antef I. He and his successors claimed to be the 'Kings of Upper and Lower Egypt' and wore clothes decorated with the symbols of both regions.

● **Despite the conflict** of the period, archaeologists have uncovered evidence that suggests not everyone felt under threat. The town of Balet was built without a fortified wall, suggesting a sense of security among the residents.

● **Art during this period** showed signs of decline. Artwork was often of a lower quality than that of the Old Kingdom.

The Middle Kingdom

- **Conflict in the First Intermediate Period** was ended by a Nebhepetra Mentuhotep. He reunited the country by conquest, heralding the start of the Middle Kingdom.

- **The Middle Kingdom** (1975–1640 BC) was a high point for art and literature. Jewellery and paintings from the period are of an exceptional quality.

- **Mentuhotep asked for shrines** to be built all over Egypt to local gods and goddesses. He also built a great memorial temple at Deir el-Bahri.

- **Mentuhotep was succeeded** by his sons. When the last of these died, his vizier Amenemhet became the founder of the 12th Dynasty.

- **The most popular king** of the 12th Dynasty was Senusret I (1965–1920 BC). Under his reign Egypt conquered part of Nubia and defeated the Libyans.

- **During the reign of Senusret III** (1818–1859 BC) several fortresses were built in Nubia. A canal was constructed to allow boats to travel around the Nile's first waterfall.

▶ *Scarab amulets were popular during the Middle Kingdom, and were worn for good fortune.*

- **During the 12th Dynasty,** pyramids were built at Dahshur and at Fayum and a new royal residence was established at el-Lisht.

- **Few of the great buildings** of the Middle Kingdom are in good condition.

- **The Middle Kingdom ended** when the Delta region was conquered by foreigners. Nubia was lost and became an independent state.

> ★ STAR FACT ★
> Queen Sobekneferu was the last ruler of the 12th Dynasty. It was very unusual at the time for a woman to rule Egypt. Her death marked the end of the golden period of the Middle Kingdom.

The Second Intermediate Period

- **During the Second Intermediate Period** (1750–1550 BC), invaders called the Hyksos settled in the Delta.

- **The Hyksos** had better weapons than the Egyptians, and overran local forces.

- **The Hyksos built** a new capital city called Avaris in 1720 BC on the ruins of the Middle Kingdom.

- **During this time,** the Theban kings of the 17th Dynasty maintained control of southern Egypt.

- **The division of Egypt** was not peaceful. The Theban king Sequenenra Taa was killed.

- **The Theban king Kamose** erected a memorial in the temple of Karnak to record his victories in battle.

▼ *The chariot provided the Hyksos people with a mobile army, which quickly overpowered the Egyptian forces.*

- **During one battle** against the Hyksos, the Theban army was led by Queen Ahhotep.

- **King Ahmose** expelled the Hyksos from Egypt and destroyed their strongholds in Palestine.

- **Under Ahmose,** the Nubian territories that were lost at the end of the Middle Kingdom were reclaimed.

> ★ STAR FACT ★
> Archaeologists have found three golden flies, awarded for valour in battle, in Queen Ahhotep's tomb.

The New Kingdom

- **The expulsion of the Hyksos** marked the beginning of the New Kingdom, which lasted from 1550–1076 BC, (18–20th Dynasties).

- **Much is known** about this period of Egyptian history because of what has been left behind.

- **With the founding** of the 18th Dynasty, the city of Waset (Thebes) became the capital of Egypt.

- **The first ruler** of the new dynasty, Ahmose, followed up his victory over the Hyksos by pursuing them into Palestine and Syria. He took territory there, before consolidating the northern borders of Egypt.

- **Ahmose's successors** built on his great military victories. The Egyptian empire grew to include parts of Palestine, Syria and most of Nubia.

- **Egypt's most successful warrior king** was Thutmose II. He led his army on 17 campaigns, conquering cities and forcing them to pay tribute (taxes) to Egypt in return for mercy.

- ◄ *Ramesses II lived to the age of 96, and was said to have had 60 daughters and 96 sons.*

- **The taxes** allowed the pharaohs to build even more temples.

- **The pharaohs of the 19th Dynasty** were descended from a vizier called Ramesses. Ramesses II became one of Egypt's most famous pharaohs.

- **Towards the end of the dynasty**, central power began to weaken again.

- **The kings of the 20th Dynasty** faced an onslaught from many directions, including the Libyans and Sea Peoples, and much of the empire was lost.

The Third Intermediate Period

- **After the fall of the 20th Dynasty,** the kings of Egypt retreated to the Delta. They had little control over the south of the country. Smendes (1069–1043 BC) became the first king of the 21st Dynasty in 1070 BC.

- **Power in Egypt** was divided between the high priests of the god Amun at Thebes in the south, and the kings of the 21st Dynasty (1070–945 BC) at Tanis in the north in Lower Egypt.

- **In the 10th century BC,** the 22nd Dynasty began in the north. Instigated by Sheshonq I (945–924 BC), these kings established a powerbase to the east of the Delta.

- **The new rulers** brought statues and obelisks (tall stone pillars) from other sites in Egypt. Archaeologists have also uncovered many gold and silver treasures in their tombs.

- **Under the rule of Takelot II** (850–825 BC), the 23rd Dynasty began. The two dynasties governed simultaneously for around 90 years.

- **By the 8th century BC,** the power in Egypt was no longer central. The 24th Dynasty had also appeared, in the form of a man called Tefnakht (724–717 BC).

- **During this period**, Nubia was ruled from the city of Napata. Although the country had its own culture, the people worshipped Egyptian gods. An independent native dynasty had begun to rule at around 760 BC.

- **The new Nubian government** extended its influence into southern Egypt. In 729 BC, Egyptian rulers Namhet and Tefnakht united to try to force out the Nubians, but their attack provoked a full-scale invasion.

- **In the 8th century BC,** King Piy of Napata, Nubia, invaded Egypt and captured all the main cities.

★ STAR FACT ★
Piy was successful in uniting Egypt. The various Egyptian leaders submitted to his rule at Memphis in 728 bc. The rule of the Nubian kings is known as the 25th Dynasty and the Late Period of Egyptian history began.

Greek-Roman Period

- **The young Macedonian king,** Alexander the Great, defeated Egypt's Persian rulers in the 4th century BC, and became Egypt's new leader.

- **Alexander incorporated** Egypt into his own empire. He founded the city of Alexandria in 332 BC, and then left Egypt to the control of two Greek officials. He died in 323 BC.

- **In 305 BC,** Alexandra's general, Ptolemy, proclaimed himself pharaoh. He founded the Ptolemaic dynasty, which lasted until 30 BC.

- **During this dynasty,** the temple of Edfu was completed and work started on the temples of Dendera, Komo Ombo and Philae.

- **During the Ptolemaic dynasty,** most important posts were held by Greeks. However, Egyptian laws and religion were largely left untouched.

- **During the Greek Period,** Ptolemy I introduced the cult of the god of Serapis in an attempt to unify Greeks and Egyptians.

> ★ **STAR FACT** ★
> Many Roman emperors commissioned temple wall paintings with themselves depicted as Egyptian pharaohs.

- **In the later Greek Period,** civil wars once again became a part of Egyptian life. Egyptians in the south tried to rebel against their foreign rulers, and there were sporadic outbreaks of violence in Alexandria.

- **In 48 BC, Roman general** Julius Caesar went to Egypt to aid Queen Cleopatra VII, who had been deposed by her brother Ptolemy XIII Philopator.

- **Cleopatra was later defeated** by the Roman leader Octavian in 30 BC. Octavian appointed himself pharaoh and Egypt became a Roman province.

▼ The Battle of Actium (31 BC) was a turning point in the history of Egypt. The Roman leader Octavian's forces repelled those of Mark Antony and Queen Cleopatra of Egypt, and forced them to flee.

The Late Period

● **Egypt's new Nubian rulers** showed great respect for the country's religion. They began a programme of repairs to the major temples and built new structures and statues to celebrate the Egyptian gods.

● **In the 7th century BC**, a new threat to Egypt emerged – Assyria. The Assyrians had tried to invade Egypt in 674 and 671 BC. The next attempt was successful, and the Nubian kings were thrown out.

● **When they had conquered Egypt,** the Assyrians sent most of their troops home, leaving an Egyptian collaborator called Nekau to run the country.

● **In the absence of Assyrians to protect him**, Nekau was murdered by Tanutamani, the last king of the 25th Dynasty. However, his victory was short-lived – he was forced to flee when the Assyrians returned.

● **When the Assyrians** were attacked by other enemies, Egypt again had an opportunity to fight for its independence.

● **The leader of the 26th Dynasty** was Psamtek I (Psammetichus) – son of the murdered Nekau. He led the Egyptians to victory against the Assyrians around 653 BC.

● **This period of ancient Egyptian history** was one of great creativity, and arts and crafts blossomed, with exquisite items made out of ceramics and bronze.

● **The country was soon invaded again,** this time by the king of Persia, and Egypt became a province of Persia. Persian kings counted as the 27th Dynasty of Egypt but there were a number of rebellions.

● **The 28th–30th Dynasties** saw a series of Egyptian leaders struggle for power. King Nectanebo II was the last native Egyptian to rule ancient Egypt.

> ★ **STAR FACT** ★
> The 26th Dynasty included some unusual rulers, such as King Amasis, who insisted that his subjects worship a statue forged out of his footbath.

What was a pharaoh?

● **The term 'pharaoh'** ('per-aa') was first used to describe the royal court, but from the time of the New Kingdom onwards it was used to refer to the king.

● **It was unusual for a woman to rule Egypt** in her own right. A queen was referred to as 'Great Royal Wife'. Hatshepsut and Nefertiti were exceptions to this rule.

● **The ancient Egyptians believed** that the pharaoh was the god Horus in human form. He represented the gods, and looked after the harmony of the universe.

● **The pharaoh was the most powerful person** in the ancient Egyptian government. He was in charge of law and order, trade and industry, and taxation.

● **To become pharaoh,** a prince had to persuade a pharaoh to employ him as 'co-regent'. When a pharaoh died, control went to his co-regent.

▶ *Queen Nefertiti was the wife of Amenhotep IV. It is thought she may have ruled in her own right, as pharaoh, after his death.*

● **The pharaoh was the religious head of state**. He was honourary high priest of every temple.

● **It was believed** that pharaohs were the only people who were allowed to approach the gods.

● **The pharaoh** was also the head of Egypt's legal system.

● **One of the duties of a pharaoh** was to protect Egypt from its enemies.

● **Some pharaohs,** such as Thutmose III, actually led the Egyptian army into battle.

The royal court and palace

- **The pharaoh and his advisers** gathered together for special state occasions.

- **Royal courts** were decorated in metals and jewels.

- **Courtiers were chosen by the pharaoh.** Ceremonies were held to dispense rewards to loyal servants.

- **If the pharaoh approached anyone** at court they had to fall before him and kiss the ground beneath his feet.

- **Dancers, jesters, magicians and musicians** kept the pharaoh entertained at court.

- **The court throne** was made of wood overlaid with gold leaf.

- **Guilds of women** were made up of the wives of officials. They reported to the goddess Hathor.

- **Some jewellery** was only allowed at certain times. A figurine of the crown could only be worn when the king was riding his chariot.

- **Only the finest materials** were used at court. Vases and plates were forged from gold, which was considered to be the most precious metal of all.

▼ *The position of dancer at the royal court was esteemed.*

Menes

- **The Egyptian historian Manetho** (305–285 BC) states that King Menes was responsible for uniting Upper and Lower Egypt and founding the First Dynasty.

- **There is a lot of uncertainty** however, as to whether King Menes actually founded the Egyptian state.

- **Some think that Manetho** is referring to a king called Horus Aha, who succeeded King Narmer.

- **Other historians** believe that Narmer and Menes were the same person, because both names have been found linked together on jar-sealings from Abydos.

- **What is certain**, is that a figure who has become known in history as King Menes founded the city of Memphis.

- **The Egyptians believed King Menes** was the first human ruler, and that the country was previously run by a succession of mythical rulers.

◀ *A scene from the tombstone of King Djet of the 1st Dynasty shows the falcon god Horus perched on top of the royal palace.*

- **During his reign**, Menes waged wars against the Nubians and Libyans in neighbouring territories.

- **During his rule**, Egyptian trade thrived. Trading with nearby countries in the Middle East appear to have been well established.

- **When Menes died**, he was succeeded by Djer. This ruler became known as 'the serpent king' because when his name was written in Egyptian script the symbols resembled a snake.

Divine symbols

▲ A scarab charm (amulet) made of green jasper that was buried with the pharaoh Sobekemsat.

● **Some symbols** were only carried by the king or queen. The ankh – the sign of life – indicated the power to give or take away life, and could not be carried by ordinary Egyptians.

● **The sphinx** was one of the most important symbols in Egypt. It was depicted with the body of a lion and the head of a pharaoh. The sphinx was a beast of the sun god, stressing the king's role as the son of Ra.

▶ The ankh symbol was based on a representation of a sandal strap.

● **The lotus flower** flourishes on the banks of the Nile. It opens its large petals with the rising of the sun. To the ancient Egyptians it represented the rebirth of the sun and the banishing of darkness.

● **The crook and flail** were carried by every Egyptian pharaoh. The crook was shaped like a shepherd's staff, and symbolized government, while the flail was shaped like a shepherd's fly-whisk, and symbolized the power of the pharaoh to punish his enemies.

● **The falcon was an important symbol**. Ra, the sun god, was most commonly represented as a falcon.

● **Bees had great religious significance** in Egypt. In one myth they were the tears of the sun god, Ra. Bees were also linked with the goddess Neith, and her temple was called 'The house of the bee'.

● **Obelisks were needle-like stone monuments**. They were based on the shape of the benben stone, upon which it was said the first rays of sunlight fell.

● **Beards were considered** to be divine attributes of the gods. Both male and female pharaohs often wore false beards secured under the chin by a cord.

● **The apis was a sacred bull**, which was chosen to live in the temple of Ptah in Memphis. Its birth was considered divine and its death provoked national mourning.

● **The large, black-green scarab dung beetle** rolls up animal droppings into a ball, which it pushes along with its head and front legs. The Egyptians associated the scarab with the god Khepri, who they believed rolled the sun across the sky every day.

◀ Jewelled falcons represented the sun god and were worn by the pharaohs.

Sneferu

- **Born in the 27th century BC**, Pharaoh Sneferu ruled Egypt for 24 years.

- **Sneferu was the son of Huni**, and the father of Khufu.

- **Sneferu was the first** pharaoh to write his name inside an oval symbol called a cartouche.

▼ *Sneferu's Bent Pyramid. This was one of two pyramids the pharaoh built at Dashur.*

- **Sneferu was a warrior.** He fought against the Nubians and the Libyans.

- **Another carving** depicts a victory at Maghara in the Sinai Peninsula.

- **Sneferu helped to finish** the pyramid at Meidum, and built the Bent Pyramid and the Red Pyramid at Dashur.

- **The three pyramids** built by Sneferu were the first attempts to construct true pyramids.

- **Sneferu placed the main axis** of his pyramids from east to west. This was an attempt to align the axis towards the passage of the sun to reflect the worship of Ra.

- **Statues of Sneferu's son** Prince Rahotep and his wife Nofret lie in the Meidum Pyramid.

- **One myth about Sneferu** tells of him ordering a court magician to roll back the waters of a lake so that the jewellery of one of his servant girls might be retrieved from its depths.

Khufu

- **Pharaoh Khufu reigned** from 2560–2537 BC. He was the son of Sneferu.

- **Khufu's greatest achievement** was the Great Pyramid at Giza, one of the Seven Wonders of the ancient world.

- **Khufu's burial treasure** was stolen by grave robbers. Only an empty coffin was found by archaeologists.

- **Part of the funerary equipment** of Khufu's mother were found in a tomb near the Great Pyramid of Giza.

- **The tomb of Khufu's son** has also been discovered at Giza to the east of the Great Pyramid.

- **Resources for the building programmes** came from trading expeditions.

- **There were also mining expeditions** into the Nubian Western desert.

- **Legend suggests** that Khufu was a tyrant, who was obsessed with building the Great Pyramid.

▶ *The Great Pyramid, the high point of building in ancient Egypt.*

- **Only one likeness of the pharaoh** survived – a statuette of a king wearing the crown of Lower Egypt.

- **The statuette was recovered** from the temple of Khentimentiu at Abydos by the explorer and artist Flinders Petrie in 1903.

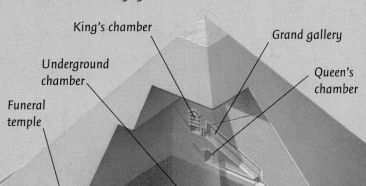

King's chamber

Grand gallery

Underground chamber

Queen's chamber

Funeral temple

Pepy II

▶ *A statue showing the young Pepy II seated on the lap of his mother, Queen Ankhnesmerire II.*

● **Pharaoh Pepy II Neferkara** succeeded the throne about 2278 BC, after his half-brother Merenra died after just nine years on the throne. Pepy II reigned for 94 years.

● **Some records suggest Pepy II** was only about 10 years old when he was appointed pharaoh.

● **Pepy II's mother** was Ankhnesmerire II (Ankhesenpepi). It is likely she acted as Pepy II's regent during his childhood, assisted by her brother, Djau, who was a vizier.

● **Texts in Harkhuf's tomb** detail the strength of Egypt's economy during Pepy II's rule. They suggest a strong economic influence over Lower Nubia.

● **Pepy II** may have been engaged in a power struggle with some of the high officials in Egypt during his reign.

● **Administration of the country** became increasingly difficult. Pepy II created the positions of vizier of Upper Egypt and vizier of Lower Egypt.

● **The last 25 years of Pepy II's reign** saw a decline in Egyptian power. The Old Kingdom ended with the death of Pepy's successor, Queen Nitiqret in 2181 BC.

● **Pepy II is buried in a pyramid** at south Saqqara. It was excavated between 1926 and 1936.

● **The pyramid contains stone statues** of bound captives in the mortuary temple, indicating that Pepy II celebrated victories by taking prisoners of war back to Egypt.

★ **STAR FACT** ★
Pepy II claimed victories over Libya that had been won by pharaoh Sahu-re. He even had Sahu-re's victory monument copied and put in his own tomb.

Amenhotep III

● **Pharaoh Amenhotep III** came to the throne when he was still a child.

● **The early years** of Amenhotep III's reign were marked by military activities.

● **The king later built a fortress** known as Khaemmaat, facing the Nubian capital over the Nile at Kerma.

● **Amenhotep had important information inscribed** on writing material called scarabs. These were sent around Egypt to broadcast news such as great military victories or successful hunts carried out by the pharaoh.

● **By the 25th year of his reign,** Amenhotep ruled a prosperous state, with great wealth from foreign trade.

● **This wealth enabled Amenhotep** to initiate much building work. Many temples were constructed or rebuilt.

● **Two of the most impressive statues** in ancient Egypt are the Colossi of Memnon, which once marked the entrance to a memorial temple at Thebes.

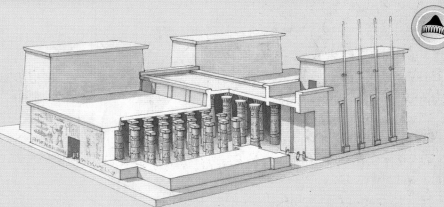

▲ *The Temple at Karnak is comprised of three main temples and several smaller structures.*

● **Under Amenhotep III**, Egypt's diplomatic ties appear to have been strengthened. Correspondence between the pharaoh and leaders in the states of Babylon, Mitanni and Arzawa was been etched onto clay tablets.

● **Amenhotep III may have been regarded as a god** (deified) during his own lifetime.

● **From the time of his first jubilee,** Amenhotep III is shown in the role of the sun god Ra, riding in his boat.

Thutmose III and Hatshepsut

- **King Thutmose III** was king during the 18th Dynasty. He was still a child, so his stepmother Hatshepsut was made queen regent.

- **After a few years as regent,** Hatshepsut had herself crowned 'King of Egypt', and remained in power for 20 years.

- **When Thutmose became king** following Hatshepsut's death, he led campaigns in Palestine and Syria.

◀ *Hatshepsut was crowned pharaoh in 1473 BC. She was very successdul, building magnificent temples and organizing new trade routes.*

- **Thutmose III's most famous victory** was a surprise attack on Megiddo, Israel.

- **Thutmose's military victories** resulted in greater wealth for Egypt.

- **In the later years of Thutmose's reign** he removed many of the images of his stepmother from Egypt's monuments.

- **Thutmose's favourite queen** was Hatshepsut-Merytre. He also had several minor queens, which he took as part of diplomatic deals.

- **Thutmose III** has a tomb in the Valley of the Kings decorated with scenes from *The Book of What is in the Underworld.*

- **In the 19th century,** archaeologists discovered Thutmose III's mummy, which had been moved to Deir el-Bahri to protect it from grave robbers.

- **At Karnak, the walls record** the many plants and animals Thutmose imported.

Akhenaten and Nefertiti

- **Pharaoh Akhenaten** was originally called Amenhotep, and was born in the 14th century BC.

- **Akhenaten ruled ancient Egypt** from around 1352 BC.

- **One of Akhenaten's projects** was the temple at Thebes, dedicated to a new god named Aten.

- **A new capital, Akhetaten,** was built at what is now Tell el-Amarna.

- **Akhenaten and Nefertiti were so devoted** to the god Aten that they prohibited the worshipping of the old gods.

- **People were made to worship** images of the pharaoh and his family being blessed by Aten.

- **Archaeologists know a lot** about ancient Egyptian life during Akhenaten's reign from the Amarna letters, which were sent to Akhenaten from rulers of the Middle East.

- **Some of the letters** tell how parts of the empire felt neglected. Others tell of plots to assassinate the king.

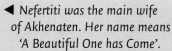

◀ *Nefertiti was the main wife of Akhenaten. Her name means 'A Beautiful One has Come'.*

- **Nobody knows what happened** to Akhenaten's body. It is likely that it was destroyed. His name was left out of the official list of kings and he was not prayed for in temples.

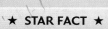

★ STAR FACT ★

Legal documents reveal just how the status of Akhenaten plummeted after his death. He became known as 'The Great Criminal'.

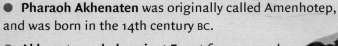
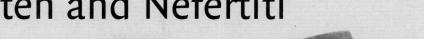

Tutankhamun

- **Pharaoh Tutankhamun was born** around 1330 BC and lived in the palace of Queen Nefertiti at Amarna.

- **Tutankhamun became king** when he was around eight years old, and married one of Akhenaten's teenage daughters.

- **Tutankhamun was responsible** for restoring the old gods that Akhenaten and Nefertiti had banned.

- **The capital was moved** back to Memphis, and high officials were buried at Saqqara once more.

- **Historians know little** of the personal life of Tutankhamun. It is thought that he had two stillborn children and that he did not survive beyond the age of 18.

- **Forensic examinations** of the king's mummy indicate that he may have been killed by a blow to the head.

- **Tutankhamun was buried** in the smallest tomb in the Valley of Kings.

- **Thousands of wonderful objects** were found crammed around Tutankhamun's tomb.

- **Tutankhamun's resting place** was a solid gold coffin with a golden funeral mask.

- **The tomb lay undisturbed** for thousands of years until it was found by Howard Carter's archaeological team in 1922.

▶ *Tutankhamun's gold coffin features a royal cobra and a vulture's head, the symbols of Lower and Upper Egypt.*

Ramesses II

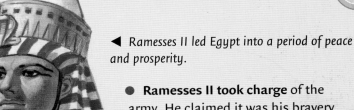

- **Eleven pharaohs were named Ramesses.** The most famous was Ramesses II (1279–1213 BC).

- **Ramesses II had several wives,** including Queen Nefertari, to whom the smaller temple of Abu Simbel was dedicated.

- **Pharaoh Ramesses was determined** to immortalize himself, and ordered the building of numerous great statues of himself.

- **An impressive temple** stood at Abu Simbel, on the Upper Nile. It was built to honour Ramesses and the gods Amun, Re-Harakhty and Ptah.

- **Another great construction** stands at Karnak – a huge temple complex that covers hundreds of acres in Luxor.

- **Ramesses II also built a new capital city** called Piramesse in the Egyptian Delta.

◀ *Ramesses II led Egypt into a period of peace and prosperity.*

- **Ramesses II took charge** of the army. He claimed it was his bravery that saved his men from destruction by the Hittites.

- **Both the Hittites and the Egyptians** claimed victory, but Ramesses decided to make peace. He married a Hittite princess as part of a peace treaty.

- **The mortuary complex** on the west bank at Thebes is known as the Ramesseum. A giant statue of the pharaoh stands there today.

- **After his death,** the mummy of Ramesses II was moved to prevent possible tomb robbers stealing it.

Alexander the Great

● **Alexander the Great** was born in 352 BC in the Greek state of Macedonia. He was the son of King Philip II and Queen Olympias, of Macedon.

● **Philip built up his army** and conquered the city of Amphipolis, Greece. He plundered this city's wealth to train soldiers and buy weapons to launch new raids into the neighbouring Thessaly and Thrace.

● **Aged 16**, Alexander was left in charge of Macedon as regent. He impressed the people of Greece with his leadership, and even led the cavalry in the battle of Chaeronea.

● **Philip was murdered four years later**, and Alexander was appointed ruler of Greece at just 20 years of age.

● **After uniting a few rebellious Greek states**, Alexander turned his attention to tackling the Persian Empire in the east, commanded by King Darius III. Its vast lands included the Egyptian Empire.

● **In the past**, Persia had successfully invaded Greece, and taken territory. This time, Alexander's forces stormed eastwards, winning battle after battle.

● **In 333 BC** Alexander's forces fought a battle at Issus with the armies of the king of Persia, Darius III. Alexander was victorious, but the Persian leader managed to escape.

● **Two years later**, the two men clashed again at Gaugamela in modern day Iraq. Again, Alexander was victorious, but once more Darius escaped. However, he was caught and deposed by his own men, and Egypt was freed from Persian rule.

● **After the Persians were ejected from Egypt**, Alexander made himself pharaoh and built a magnificent new city called Alexandria. His tomb is thought to be there, but has not yet been discovered.

> ★ STAR FACT ★
> Today, Alexandria is still the second largest city in Egypt, and the country's main port, just as Alexander the Great had planned. It is laid out like a Greek city of the time, with a grid street plan.

▶ *Alexander the Great was carried by his beloved horse Bucephalus into many of the battles that helped forge his great empire.*

Cleopatra VII

- **Cleopatra VII ruled Egypt** from 51 BC with her half-brother Ptolemy XIII.

- **Ptolemy forced his sister** out of power, so Cleopatra called on Roman general Julius Caesar.

- **Julius Caesar** made Cleopatra queen. She had to share the throne with another brother, Ptolemy XIV.

- **Cleopatra gave birth to a son.** She called him Caesarion, and claimed that Caesar was his father.

- **When her half-brother died,** Cleopatra made Caesarion her co-ruler.

- **Cleopatra is famous** for her love affair with the Roman general Mark Antony.

- **Cleopatra used her wealth** to pay for Mark Anthony's armies. In return, Mark Antony made Alexandria the capital of a new independent Egyptian empire.

- **Antony had acted** without permission from the Roman government, so fighting soon erupted. Antony and Cleopatra were defeated at the battle of Actium.

- **Antony killed himself** when Octavian closed in upon Alexandria. Cleopatra committed suicide soon afterwards. Caesarion was murdered and Egypt was incorporated into the Roman Empire.

- **Cleopatra's palace** has been found underwater at Alexandria.

▶ *The marriage of Cleopatra and Mark Antony hastened the end of Egypt's independence.*

Arrival of the Romans

- **After the battle of Actium,** the Romans took control of Egypt. Emperor Octavian made himself pharaoh.

- **Roman law was implemented in Egypt.** Egyptian farmers were taxed and much of their produce went to Rome.

- **The Romans mined gold** and precious stones from the desert to provide wealth for their empire.

- **Egypt was important** to the Romans because the land produced so much food.

- **Life for the poor** was often harsh in Roman-controlled Egypt, and there were several uprisings.

- **Many Romans settled in Egypt,** and some adopted Egyptian culture.

★ STAR FACT ★
Tourism became popular at this time. Graffiti describes how people liked to visit the ancient monuments of Memphis and Thebes.

- **People buried during this period** were placed in an Egyptian-style coffin, but with a Roman-style portrait instead of a mummy mask.

- **Archaeologists have uncovered** letters from the Roman period of Egyptian history, which give useful information about people's lives.

- **The Romans built temples.** Names of emperors such as Augustus (Octavian) are inscribed on the walls of temples at Dakka and Dendera.

◀ *Later in his reign, Octavian took the name Augustus, which means 'respected one'.*

Christian Egypt

- **Some historians** believe that Christianity was established in Egypt by Mark the Evangelist around AD 33.

- **By AD 200**, Alexandria was one of the great Christian centres in the world.

◀ *Emperor Constantine had a vision in which he was told that he should conquer new lands on behalf of Jesus Christ.*

- **The form of Christianity** that emerged became known as Coptic Christianity. It still survives today.

- **Early Christian** shields had illustrations of the god Horus on horseback, representing warrior saints.

- **Once the new religion** had spread throughout the empire, the old pagan temples became churches, houses or monasteries.

- **One of St Mark's first converts** iwas the shoemaker Anianus, who went on to become a bishop of Alexandria.

- **Early Christians** faced terrible persecution in Roman-ruled Egypt.

- **In AD 64 Emperor Nero** made it an offence to profess the Christian faith.

- **During the rule of Emperor Diocletian**, 284 Egyptian Christians were executed in a single year.

- **After that, persecutions started to dwindle** and Egypt became a Christian state when the Roman Empire converted to Christianity under Constantine in AD 325.

Muslim and Ottoman Egypt

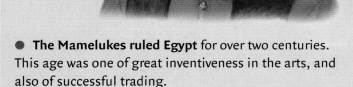

- **Arab armies conquered Egypt** in the 7th century AD.

- **Islam was made the state religion** of Egypt. A succession of Muslim leaders were appointed to rule.

- **In 1171 Salah-ed-Din** (Saladin) took control of Egypt by force and made himself sultan, founding the Ayyubid dynasty (1171–1250).

- **Men in Islamic Egypt** were forbidden to wear gold by their religion, so they wore jewellery made from other materials.

- **Saladin was a warlord** who reconquered most of Syria and Palestine.

- **In the 12th century**, Cairo faced attacks from Christian crusaders. Saladin ordered that the city be fortified.

- **The city's fortifications** failed to reassure al-Kamil, so he hired an army of Turkish soldiers – the Mamelukes – to defend Cairo. However, the Mamelukes decided to seize power for themselves.

▶ *By the end of Sultan Selim's rule, control of Egypt had passed to the Ottoman Empire.*

- **The Mamelukes ruled Egypt** for over two centuries. This age was one of great inventiveness in the arts, and also of successful trading.

- **By the early 16th century** the rule of the Mamelukes was failing. The Ottoman Sultan Selim I invaded Egypt in 1517. The country became part of the Ottoman Empire.

- **Egypt was governed by a pasha**, appointed by the sultan. But the power of the Ottoman Empire began to decline.

Colonial Egypt

● **In 1798, the French leader** Napoleon Bonaparte landed in Egypt. He defeated the Mameluke army in the Battle of the Pyramids, but his fleet was in turn defeated by the British, led by Admiral Nelson. The French left Egypt just three years later.

● **In this period of confusion** Mohammad Ali, an officer of Albanian descent, came forward to take control of Egypt. He was given the title of 'pasha' by the Ottoman sultan in 1801 and initiated a programme of modernization.

● **Ali began eradicating all Mameluke influence** in Egypt. He also conquered Sudan, Palestine and Syria – though he failed in his efforts to conquer Greece.

● **In 1831** European forces intervened to prevent Ali overthrowing the sultan of Turkey but the Egyptian leader gained control of Syria and Crete.

> ★ STAR FACT ★
> The first efforts to build a modern canal came from the Egyptian expedition of Napoleon Bonaparte, who hoped the project would create a trade problem for the English.

● **After the death of Ali**, control of Egypt passed to his nephew Abbas in 1848, and then to his sons Said (1854––1863) and Ismail (1863–1879). During the reign of Ismail, the Suez Canal was opened.

● **By the end of the 19th century** the country was in debt. In 1876, an Anglo-French commission was put in charge of Egypt's finances. Ismail was removed by the Sultan for incompetence and his son Tawfik Pasha was put in charge. When the Egyptian army rebelled, Tawfik issued a direct appeal to Britain for help. In response, they occupied Egypt in 1882.

● **Although British forces** did succeed in re-establishing order in Egypt, their presence was bitterly resented. In 1918, the Wafd, an Egyptian nationalist party led by Saad Zaghlul, demanded independence. In 1922, Britain reluctantly retreated from Egypt.

● **After the removal of the British**, King Fuad I established Egypt's first constitution as a parliamentary monarchy.

● **Egypt joined** the League of Nations in 1937.

▶ Work began on the Suez canal in 1859, and the project was completed in 1867. The canal saves ships a 7700-km detour through dangerous seas.

Egypt today

● **Egypt became a republic** on 18 June 1953, when King Farouk abdicated. Colonel Gamel Abdel Nasser was made prime minister, and later, president.

● **President Nasser** embarked on a series of projects including the construction of the Aswan High Dam.

● **In 1958**, Egypt founded the United Arab Republic with Yemen and Syria. In 1967 they engaged in the Six Day War with Israel.

● **After the Six Day War**, Egypt was forced to recognize Israel. Egypt's occupied regions were returned.

● **Nasser's successor**, Anwar al-Sadat, launched an attack against Israeli occupiers in Sinai in 1973. The Egyptians were forced back, and a ceasefire agreement was reached.

● **In 1978** the Camp David Agreement was signed. Israel withdrew from Sinai, and Egypt recognized Israel.

● **On 6 October 1981,** Sadat was assassinated. His successor, Hosni Mubarak, has been in power ever since.

● **Under Mubarak,** Egypt has become close to the West, sending troops to fight against Iraq in the Gulf War.

● **Recently, Egypt has been targeted** by Islamic fundamentalists. In 1997 a bus of holiday-makers was fired on as it visited the temple of Hatshepsut.

● **Despite unrest,** Egypt continues to thrive, and the economy is booming.

▼ *The bustling city of Cairo today is home to over 15 million people. Its official name is Al-Qahirah.*

Food and drink

● **Most of what we know** about the ancient Egyptian diet comes from scenes painted in tombs.

● **The average Egyptian table** would have boasted meats, fish, vegetables and fruits.

● **Meat such as sheep**, poultry, oxen and antelope were eaten by ancient Egyptians. Meat was expensive, and the poor often ate fish instead.

● **Major trading routes** passed through Egypt, bringing exotic eastern spices.

● **The Egyptians grew grapes** which were eaten or made into wine. Wine was also made from dates. Beer made from barley was more widely available.

● **Dates and honey** were used as sweeteners. Bees were kept in pottery hives.

◄ *Wall art in tombs depicts rich Egyptians enjoying delicacies such as butter, cheese, fowl and beef.*

● **Wall paintings** show workers baking bread in flat moulds. Cakes were made using fruits such as dates and figs.

● **Kitchen utensils** included bowls, pans, ladles and whisks. Ordinary Egyptians used dishes made from clay, while the rich used dishes of gold, silver or bronze.

● **The kitchen was in the courtyard** or on the roof. Ancient Egyptians cooked in clay ovens or charcoal fires.

● **An ancient papyrus** indicates what the Egyptians considered to be special foods. The hero of *The Story of the Shipwrecked Sailor* delighted in figs, grapes, fish and birds.

Fashion

● **The ancient Egyptians** cut their hair short to cope with the heat and the wealthy dressed up in black wigs made from wool or human hair for special occasions.

● **Make-up was used** by rich and poor. Men and women applied kohl as eyeliner, and powdered ochre to flush the cheeks.

● **Fashion-conscious Egyptians** could study themselves in mirrors made from copper or bronze. Good glass was scarce.

● **Poor Egyptians wore** rings and bracelets of cheap metals and clay. The rich wore gold and precious stones.

▶ *Clothing was light and loose-fitting, because of the scorching climate.*

● **The hot climate** dictated that clothing was light, made from linen. Men wore linen loin cloths, fastened round the waist, while women wore long, tunic-type dresses.

● **Shoes were often made of papyrus**. They were usually simple sandals similar to flip-flops.

● **Cleanliness was very important** for Egyptian women. Wealthier women used a cleansing paste of water and natron, a compound found in sodium bicarbonate.

● **Egyptian women rubbed oils into their skin** after washing, possibly fragranced with frankincense or myrrh.

● **Influences from the Middle East** probably led to ear piercing. By the 14th century BC, many Egyptian men and women wore large earrings.

Women in society

● **The most important posts** in ancient Egypt were filled by men. Women were expected to look after the home.

● **Women performed many of the agricultural tasks** in ancient Egypt.

● **Egyptian women** were usually free to go about in public without an escort.

▼ *Richer households had servants to help with tasks ranging from getting dressed to cleaning.*

● **Egyptian women** were allowed to own possessions and property. They were usually given as gifts or inherited.

● **Under Egyptian property law**, a woman had claim to one-third of all the property the couple had acquired during their marriage.

● **If a woman brought private property** to a marriage it remained hers. In the event of divorce her property was returned to her, plus any divorce settlement.

● **If a wife was badly treated,** she could divorce her husband. She was then free to marry again.

● **Most women** looked after their family and home, but some acted as housekeepers, servants, or skilled labourers.

● **Women were not usually taught** how to read and write.

● **Women could be national heroines.** Queen Ahhotep of the 18th Dynasty became a legend for saving Egypt from the Hyksos, receiving Egypt's highest military decoration at least three times.

Family and marriage

- **Several generations of Egyptians** shared a home. Servants and slaves were often considered to be part of the family.

- **The head of the household** was always a man. His wife was called the 'mistress of the house'.

- **Marriage was quite informal.** Marriage contracts were only used from the Late Period.

- **Marriages usually took place** between people of the same social class.

- **Children were central** to family life, and married couples were expected to have several children.

- **A prospective husband** paid a sum of money to the bride's father. Later this practice was reversed.

- **Some houses were fitted with false doors** (*mastabas*) to allow the spirits of dead relatives to visit.

- **Many statues and wall paintings** suggest that ordinary Egyptians had lifelong marriages to only one partner.

◀ On her wedding day, the bride wore a long linen dress or tunic. Gold, silver or gems such as lapis lazuli were also worn by richer women.

- **Girls from poor families** married at 12. Boys were usually working before they married, so rarely wed before the age of 15. In royal marriages, the participants were often much younger.

- **The elderly were treated with great respect.** Small figures of dead ancestors were often kept around the house.

Children

- **Children were considered a blessing.** If a couple could not have their own children, they could adopt.

- **Disease and accidents** claimed the lives of one out of every two or three births. To compensate, families had on average four to six children, and some had as many as 15.

- **The ancient Egyptians** had tests for determining a woman's fertility. A woman sprinkled her own urine onto wheat and barley. If the barley grew, it was believed she would have a boy; if the wheat grew, a girl. If neither grew, the woman would not have children.

- **The chief goddess** of childbirth was the hippopotamus goddess, Taweret. Women placed an ivory wand on their stomachs to ask for her help.

- **Childbirth was dangerous**, and many women died during it.

- **A child was usually named immediately** and then registered with the Egyptian authorities.

- **Babies were nursed by their mothers** for about three years, carried around in a sling around her neck to allow her to carry on working.

- **From the age of five**, children began helping their parents to earn a living or run the household.

- **Children were expected** to perform tasks such as assisting with the harvest or running errands.

- **In the poorest families**, the fate of children was not so pleasant. They might be given away to work in temples or sold as slaves.

◀ Toys and games have been found by archaeologists, as well as paintings showing children playing.

Education

● **Few Egyptians** received any formal education. Most were illiterate, and received vocational training aimed at preparing them for their future employment. Skills such as carpentry were passed on through generations.

● **Schooling was very expensive**, and many families were unable to afford it. The ability to read and write could sometimes lead to being given a position as a scribe, which was one of the most coveted jobs in Egypt.

● **To become a scribe**, you went to a special school at the age of about nine. Training took between 7 and 12 years to complete. Only then were scribes allowed to write on papyrus scrolls.

★ **STAR FACT** ★
There was no set number of years at school. One man recorded that he started school aged five. At the age of 16 he was appointed a wab priest. After 39 years he was appointed high priest.

● **Students made their own brushes** and colours and copied out long lists of words and phrases. They then progressed to copying whole texts.

● **The texts** were usually moral works, packed full of advice about how a young Egyptian should behave.

● **There were many employment options** for scribes. You could seek work in a temple, a law court, within the government, or as a travelling war reporter with the Egyptian army.

● **The ancient Egyptians** believed that writing was sacred – a skill given to them by the god of wisdom, Thoth.

● **Schools were attached to temples** and government offices. Royal children had their own schools inside palaces.

● **Education seems to have been** almost entirely restricted to men. There is evidence of only one girl being taught to read and write – a 20th Dynasty letter from a man to his son says, 'You shall see that daughter of Khonsumose and let her make a letter and send it to me.'

▲ *Learning how to write was a very laborious process that was restricted to children from only the richest families. Would-be scribes were sent to special schools to learn their trade.*

Politics and government

- **The ancient Egyptians** have left much evidence about the way their country was governed and administered. Written and archaeological sources reveal the supply and demand of items such as grain.

- **Everything that went on in government was noted down** by scribes. Documents recovered include wills, title deeds, census lists, conscription lists, orders, memos, tax lists and letters.

- **The most important person** in Egypt after the pharaoh was the vizier (prime minister).

- **The vizier was responsible** for overseeing the development of royal monuments and for registering people and property for tax purposes.

- **Scribes were crucial** in all aspects of government, from assessing taxes to compiling war reports.

- **Foreign affairs were managed** by the governors of foreign provinces. Diplomats travelled between countries.

★ STAR FACT ★
Egyptian society was hierarchical, with the pharaoh at the top, and the peasant workers and slaves at the bottom.

- **Egypt was governed locally** by a series of administrative districts called *nomes*. There were 42 nomes in total. Each nome was governed by a figure appointed by the pharaoh. They were called nomarchs.

- **It was possible to overcome class barriers** and reach high office from a humble background.

- **By the time of the New Kingdom** national administration was divided into three parts – the dynasty, internal administration and external affairs.

- **Internal administration** was split into four parts – the royal domain, the army and navy, religious hierarchy and civil officials.

Law and order

- **The prevention of crime** was the responsibility of local officials.

- **Cases were constructed** against suspects by interrogation, re-enactments, and checking records.

- **There do not seem to** have been any written laws or any lawyers. Cases were tried by groups of judges.

- **Pharaohs maintained justice on Earth** because they were believed to be the living embodiment of the gods.

- **The head of the Egyptian legal system** was the vizier. Courts were run by magistrates.

- **The office of a judge** or magistrate was very highly regarded, and became a valued profession.

- **Egyptians brought before court** often represented themselves. Their previous record was taken into account by the judge.

- **Stealing and receiving stolen goods** were common crimes in ancient Egypt.

▲ Maat was the goddess of law and truth, represented as a woman with an ostrich-feather crown. Judges wore an image of her, such as a pendant on a necklace.

- **A confession was basis for a conviction** in court. The methods by which this confession was achieved were deemed irrelevant.

★ STAR FACT ★
Police patrols used dogs, and occassionally, trained monkeys!

Punishments

- **Punishments were severe** in Egyptian society. Forgers had their hands cut off, and disobedient soldiers were asked to make amends by performing heroic deeds.

- **The official penalty** for grave robbers was to be burnt alive or to be impaled on a stake and left to die.

- **Offenders were sometimes banished** to a remote oasis in the desert.

- **Many Egyptians believed** that if you escaped punishment on Earth you would be punished during the afterlife.

- **There were no long-term prisons** in Egypt. Criminals were sentenced to time in labour camps.

- **Punishments were often extended** to the offender's family. If a man committed the crime of desertion, he could be imprisoned along with his entire family.

- **The names of King Teti's bodyguards** were scratched from their graves because they were said to have assassinated him.

▶ *Punishment for the crime of tax evasion was harsh.*

- **The ancient Egyptians believed** that spirits could be punished.

- **A spirit found guilty of being an enemy of Ra** could be boiled in a cauldron or burned in a lake of fire.

- **Thieves could register their profession** and declare their earnings.

Tomb robbers

- **Grave looting** probably began soon after the practice of burying the rich with their possessions began.

- **Old Kingdom inscriptions** contained warnings that robbers would be judged by the gods in the next life.

- **Tomb builders** devised measures such as hidden chambers to try to stop thieves.

- **The pyramid** of the 12th Dynasty king, Amenemhat III at Hawara, had blind passages and trapdoors.

- **Amenpenofer, a builder working for Amenhotep,** organized a robbery of the pyramid of Sobekmesef. They collected the valuables and burned the remains.

- **Howard Carter noted** at least two robberies of Tutankhamun's tomb.

- **Despite the wealth found by Carter,** most of the pharaoh's treasure had probably gone.

- **Some robberies** may have been committed even before the deceased was buried.

- **The Egyptians believed** that provisions were necessary for the deceased to survive the afterlife, so it is surprising that some Egyptians were willing to deprive their ancestors of this right by robbing tombs.

- **It is likely that thieves** may have been in league with undertakers and cemetery guardians.

◀ *Nearly every tomb in ancient Egypt has been looted.*

The army

- **There was no permanent army** in the Old Kingdom. Forces were conscripted for specific expeditions.

- **Until Lower Egypt was conquered** by the Hyksos people in 1674 BC, Egypt had never fought a large-scale war with another country.

- **The Egyptian army** had become professional by the time of the 17th and 18th Dynasties of the New Kingdom, and the army became dominated by noblemen.

- **From this period onwards**, specialized units began to evolve. These ranged from trench diggers to units armed with battering rams and groups of Nubian archers.

- **The pharaoh** or his son was usually in charge of the army. Ranks were similar to those in the modern army.

- **The armies** of ancient Egypt were tiny in comparison to modern armies.

- **A division** contained several thousand men. These would be divided into battalions of 500 soldiers, and subdivided into 250 platoons of 50 men.

- **An Egyptian army's tactics** were usually to march in divisions towards the enemy lines. It was hoped that sheer weight of numbers would prevail.

- **From the Old Kingdom onwards**, mercenaries (soldiers available for hire) were recruited. By the time of the latter part of the New Kingdom, mercenaries formed the majority of the forces.

- **Army divisions** were named after gods such as Amun. Appeals were made to the god of the province to boost the spirits of the soldiers.

▶ Ancient Egyptian soldiers would have carried stone or bronze weapons such as spears, axes and daggers. Shields were made first from turtle shells, and then from leather.

Egypt's neighbours

- **Nubia offered Egypt** a trading route into Africa, and wealth through its gold mines. Egyptian activity in Nubia dates back to 3500 BC.

- **The nomadic tribes of Libya** periodically raided the western Delta and the desert oases.

- **In the Second Intermediate Period**, Egypt was invaded by the Hyksos people. They ruled until they were driven out by Egyptian kings from Thebes.

- **The Thebean kings** faced an uneasy relationship with the Hittites. Ramesses II subdued them at Qadesh, and later signed a peace treaty with them.

- **The Sea People** were migrant groups looking for land. In 1177 BC they attacked Egypt, but were crushed by the armies of Ramesses III.

- **The Assyrians** attacked Egypt in the 7th century BC.

- **Under Alexander the Great,** Egypt became part of the Greek Empire in 332 BC.

- **Egypt was incorporated** into the Roman Empire in 30 BC. The Roman emperor Octavian became pharaoh.

- **The chief exports** of ancient Egypt were linen, papyrus and grain.

- **The Egyptians traded** their goods for silver, copper, olive oil, cedar and lapis lazuli.

▶ Conquered peoples paid homage to the pharaoh by bringing gifts.

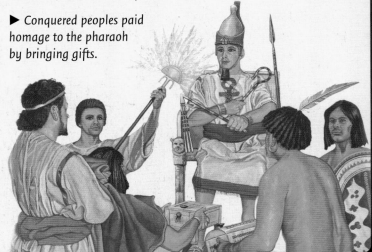

Towns and cities

● **Most Egyptian towns** were built on raised land, far enough away from the Nile to minimize flooding, but close enough to allow access to water.

● **Memphis was Egypt's first capital**, probably founded by King Narmer in about 3100 BC after the unification of Upper and Lower Egypt.

● **Thebes first became important** during the Middle Kingdom when the 11th Dynasty kings made it their capital. During the New Kingdom, a number of kings were buried in rock-cut tombs in the Valley of the Kings. Queens, princes and princesses were buried in the Valley of the Queens.

● **El-Amarna**, on the east bank of the Nile between Minya and Asyaut, is the most complete city to have survived. It was founded by Akhenaten during the New Kingdom.

● **Alexandria was founded** in the 4th century BC by the Greek general Alexander the Great, who envisaged the city as the centre of his empire. It was laid out on a grid system like a Greek city, and divided into districts.

● **A number of towns** were built around specific trades. A workers' village was built at Giza. It was constructed to house the men who laboured over Khufu's pyramid.

● **The town of Illahun** (Kahun) was discovered by Flinders Petrie. It once housed the workers that built the pyramid of King Senusret.

● **Fortress towns** were built in Egyptian-controlled Nubia from the Middle Kingdom onwards. Buhen, 250 km south of Aswan, was constructed on an Old Kingdom site, surrounded by a mud-brick enclosure wall.

● **At the height** of the ancient Egyptian civilization there were about 17 cities and 24 towns governed by the capital. Their estimated population was between 100,000 and 200,000. Small towns had up to 3000 inhabitants, while Memphis and Thebes had up to 40,000.

● **Craftworkers, scribes**, priests and shopkeepers lived and worked in cities, while farmers and herdsmen left the towns to travel to the countryside to work each day.

▼ *The town of Deir el-Medina lay in a valley on the west bank across from Luxor. It was built to house the workers who constructed the royal tombs in the Valley of the Kings.*

Weapons and warfare

- **During the Old Kingdom**, Egyptian soldiers used a variety of weapons, including spears, daggers and axes.

- **The bow and arrow** was the most important weapon. The earliest metal arrowheads date from around 2000 BC.

- **The first arrowheads** were made of flint or wood.

- **Archery units** were deadlier when used with the chariot, introduced around 3000 BC by the Sumerians.

- **Operating a bow and arrow** was difficult, and specialist equipment protected the archer.

- **The sling required** considerable skill to be effective. Pebbles, and later lead, were used as missiles.

- **Armour was light.** Pharaohs may have worn armour inlaid with semi-precious stones.

- **During the New Kingdom**, soldiers carried spears, axes and daggers. Thutmose III was one of the first Egyptians to use a scimitar – a deadly curved sword.

- **Egyptian war galleys** (boats) were used to carry men and supplies to battlegrounds. Some were fitted with battering rams.

- **During peacetime**, weapons were kept in royal armouries. When Egypt was at war, they were distributed in lavish ceremonies.

◀ *Chariots were used as fast-moving vehicles from which archers could launch deadly attacks.*

A soldier's life

- **Egyptian soldiers lived together** in compounds based around forts. Donkeys were used to carry army supplies.

- **Camps were rectangular**, protected by a fence of leather shields. The king had a separate tent in the centre.

- **Scribes organized the logistics** of supplying such a huge number of men.

- **Camp life** was run on a system of rationing. Conscripts were registered, then allocated rations. They were paid in food or tokens according to experience.

- **When the Egyptians began a campaign**, they prayed to the gods for protection.

- **A mast on the pharaoh's chariot** carried a symbol of the sun representing Amun-Ra, king of the gods.

- **Awards were granted** for valiant service. Land, slaves and other goods were distributed among brave soldiers.

- **As the Egyptian army grew reliant** on mercenaries, it became vulnerable to desertion and rebellions.

▶ *Many Egyptian rulers believed that the king of the gods, Amun-Ra, fought with them in battle.*

- **A talented soldier** could increase his position in society through his achievements in battle. Several army commanders became kings – notably Horemheb and Ramesses I.

- **Necklaces with golden flies** or bees were awarded to men who had excelled in combat by persistently 'stinging' Egypt's foes.

Flowers and trees

Date

- **Egyptians believed** that flowers had special properties, and that their scent came from the gods. Incense from flowers was used at funerals and in temple rituals.

- **Men and women wore perfumes** made from lilies and lotus flowers. Collars and headdresses of petals were worn on special occasions.

- **Flowers were often symbolic.** Papyrus represented prosperity and the unity of Upper and Lower Egypt.

- **Trees provided shade** from the sun. Species such as palm grew readily in the Nile Valley, providing fruit, wood and shelter.

- **Olive trees** were grown around temples. They provided a source of oil for the lamps that were used at the shrines.

- **Good quality wood** was not readily available. Most native species were small and slow-growing, such as acacia and sycamore. They were of little use for building.

Raffia palm

◄ *Date palm trees were grown in the gardens of nobles. It was believed they increased a person's lifespan.*

- **Wood was imported** from the Old Kingdom onwards, including cedar and pine from the Lebanon and ebony from Africa.

- **The ancient Egyptians** associated many trees with gods and the afterlife. Hathor was referred to as the 'lady of the sycamore'.

- **Trees were sometimes linked** with the duration of a pharaoh's rule. Reliefs have been found showing the gods Thoth and Seshat inscribing the leaves of the ished tree with the number of years in a pharaoh's reign.

- **The symbol of a date palm branch** was used in hieroglyphs to denote the word 'year'.

Animals

- **The banks of the Nile** were home to many different birds, beasts, fish and reptiles.

- **The importance of animals** is shown by the number of gods and goddesses with animal features. There were also cults devoted to sacred animals.

- **The Egyptians kept** domesticated cattle, sheep, goats, pigs, geese and horses. Animals were a source of food, clothing and labour. The cow was sacred to many goddesses. Bulls were sacred to Ra.

- **Horses did not become common** until the New Kingdom. The Hyksos introduced them during the Second Intermediate Period.

- **Many different animals** were kept as pets. Evidence has been discovered of domesticated geese, cats, dogs and even monkeys.

◄ *Many mummified dogs have been found across Egypt. Dog cemeteries have been discovered in Hardai.*

▶ *From the Late Period, great numbers of cats were mummified. Many bronze statues were also made.*

- **Wild cats** were domesticated during the Middle Kingdom. They were regarded as pets but were also sacred to the goddess Bastet.

- **Dogs were not regarded** as highly as cats. Some Egyptians clearly formed attachments with their dogs, but the term 'dog' was commonly used as an insult.

- **Hippos and crocodiles** lurked in the waters of the Nile. There were also lions, cheetahs, hyenas, jackals, wolves, cobras and wild cattle.

- **The Nile was a haven for bird life**. It was home to such birds as the falcon, kite, goose, crane, ibis, vulture, plover and owl.

- **The Nile teemed with many varieties of fish**. In some places certain types of fish were sacred, but in other places the same fish were a source of food.

Buying and selling

- **Trade took place** through bartering – goods were swapped for items of equivalent value instead of money.

- **Sales records** give information on rates of exchange. The value of goods depended on their availability.

- **At market places** in towns and villages, people met to swap goods. They were also frequented by travelling salesmen looking to pick up merchandise.

- **Foreign coins** were introduced in the 5th century BC. In the 4th century BC the Egyptians began to mint their own coins.

- **Lending money** was common. Sometimes these were official loans with interest rates.

- **As early as the Pre-Dynastic Period**, merchants were buying exotic items to bring into Egypt, including leopard skins, ivory and gold.

- **The army organized** international trading expeditions. These were often dangerous. Hatshepsut's expedition to Punt took over three years.

- **Historians** are not exactly sure where the land of Punt was. It is thought to have been in the region of the river Atbara in what is now Ethiopia.

- **The ancient Egyptians** traded with the adjacent countries along the Mediterranean Sea and the Nile River to the south. They set up trade routes to Cyprus, Crete, Greece, Syro-Palestine, Punt and Nubia.

- **Greek traders** were regular visitors to Egypt, and were permitted to set up their own town in the Nile Delta.

◀ Egyptian workers carried their oil to market. It would then be exchanged for goods they needed.

Building the pyramids

- **The Great Pyramid at Giza** was built using over 2 million stone blocks, each weighing 2.5 tonnes.

- **Pyramids required a site** on the west bank of the Nile, close to the river, but also above flood level.

- **After the ground was levelled**, the next task was to calculate true north, so that the sides of the pyramid could be lined up with the four compass points.

- **A pharaoh** blessed the foundations before work began. He performed sacred rites including marking out the foundations, cutting earth and moulding the first brick.

- **Ensuring the stone blocks** were smooth was the job of the masons. They used tools called boning rods – two handles joined by a sharp cutting cord.

- **The core of the pyramid** and the outer casing were limestone. Granite was used for chambers and passages. Sculptures were made from sandstone.

- **Egyptologists** have found tools left by pyramid workers, including rock drills, clamps and chisels.

- **A huge army** of workers built the Great Pyramid, most of them farmers.

- **Historians believe** teams of builders used sledges to drag the stones into position.

- **The workers** probably laid logs across the ramp to make the sledges easier to move.

▶ Stone slabs were hauled up to the pyramid site using sledges and ramps.

Servants and slavery

● **Most slaves** in ancient Egypt were prisoners of war or foreigners. Occasionally, poor Egyptians were forced to sell their children into slavery.

● **A slave had some legal rights.** They could marry a free person and own property.

● **A slave could be employed** to perform tasks ranging from manual labour to government administration.

● **Foreign female slaves** were employed in Egyptian homes to do housework or make clothes.

● **Egyptian slaves could buy or work** their way to freedom. They could hold important positions in government.

● **Slaves were often given as presents**, or could be left in a will to family members.

● **Sometimes slaves were freed** by their owners. It was not unknown for some slaves to then be adopted by the family of their former owner.

● **Ownership of slaves** was not restricted to the elite.

● **Films depicting slaves** building pyramids are inaccurate. Most pyramid building was done by farmers.

● **During the Pre-Dynastic Period,** if the pharaoh died, his slaves would be buried alive with him along with the rest of his possessions.

◀ *Servants were responsible for everything from cooking and cleaning to helping their masters and mistresses get dressed in the morning.*

Doctors

● **Egyptian doctors** were famed throughout the ancient world. They used magic and medicine to treat patients.

● **Illness was often regarded** as the result of evil spirits. Doctors would often work with a magician.

● **Prayers to the gods** (especially to Sekhmet, the goddess of healing) were in some cases accompanied by the injection of medicines into the ears or nostrils.

● **It was thought that plants** had both medicinal and magical properties.

● **The ancient equivalents of doctors** were called 'sinws'. There were also surgeons, called 'priests of Sekhmet', and dental practitioners. Doctors were always male.

● **Egyptian doctors** gave out prescriptions. Medical records listing 876 prescriptions for complaints such as stomach problems and skin irritations have been found.

● **Doctors weighed** out the ingredients of medicines according to a system known as 'the eye of Horus'.

● **People's teeth** were usually in poor condition. Dentists prescribed opium to treat severe pain.

● **Doctors were expected** to treat cosmetic problems. They prescribed lotions for skin care, and ointments and remedies to stop hair loss.

● **People wore magical charms** or amulets thought to ward off sickness.

▶ *An Egyptian doctor applies a herbal preparation to a sick patient.*

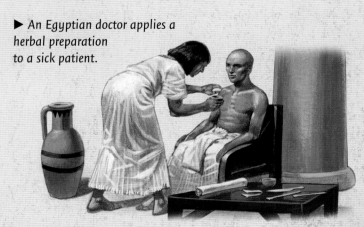

Gods

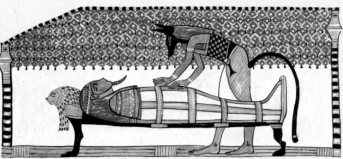

▶ Anubis was the canine god of the dead. He was associated with the mummification process, and was the guardian of burial places.

● **Hundreds of gods** were worshipped by the ancient Egyptians. The Egyptian word for 'god' was denoted by a flagpole sign in ancient Egyptian script.

● **The sun god Ra** was the most important god. He could take many forms, including Khepri (a scarab beetle) and Re-Harakhty (a great hawk).

● **The Egyptians believed** Ra created everything on Earth, as well as the underworld and the other gods. Ra was king of the gods and protector of the pharaoh. He was usually shown as a falcon-headed man wearing a sun disc.

● **The moon god Thoth** was the god of writing, medicine and mathematics.

● **Osiris, god of the dead**, represented the resurrection into eternal life that Egyptians sought by having their corpses embalmed.

● **The pharaoh** was thought to be the embodiment of the god Horus. This hawk-headed god was the child of Osiris and Isis.

● **Seth, the red god**, was the god of chaos. He was the embodiment of evil.

● **Ptah was the chief god** of Memphis. The Egyptians believed that he created the Moon, the Sun and the Earth.

● **Bes was a dwarf god** who was believed to guard against evil spirits and bad luck.

● **Khnum was a god of fertility** and creation. With a ram's head and horns, he guarded the source of the Nile.

Goddesses

● **Isis was the goddess** of fertility and nature.

● **Sekhemet was the goddess of love** and protection. Doctors and other healers prayed for her aid. She was depicted as a lioness.

● **Hathor, daughter of the sun god Ra**, was goddess of the sky and of love, mirth and beauty.

● **The Two Ladies** were fierce goddesses called Wadjyt and Nekhbet. They defended the sun god and the pharaohs against enemies.

● **The cat goddess Bastet** was the daughter of Ra. Her main temple was in the Delta region, where archaeologists discovered a cemetery full of mummified cats.

● **Taweret was depicted** as part lion, part hippopotamus and part crocodile. She was a kind and generous figure who protected women and children.

● **Nut was the sky goddess**. She was depicted as a nude or as a giant cow.

◀ Bastet was a cat goddess who was thought to be the daughter of the sun god. She was often depicted as a woman with the head of a lioness, and later simply as a cat-headed woman.

● **Nut also protected the dead** and assisted in their rebirth.

● **The goddess Neith** was thought to have made order and chaos, and good and evil. Her blessing often appears on shrouds and mummy bandages.

● **Nephythys was a child** of the earth god Keb and the sky goddess Nut. She was believed to be the goddess of the dead, and appeared as a woman or as a small bird of prey.

Priests

- **The pharaoh was the high priest** of Egypt, and the only priest allowed to be depicted in the temples. Thousands of lesser priests were employed to look after the temples.

- **A priest's main role** was to care for the temple. Scribes were usually appointed as priests, and in many cases the position became hereditary.

- **The pharaoh was supported** by the chief priest, or 'first prophet'. The 'second prophets' looked after the economy of the temple. The lower orders (wab priests) looked after more menial duties such as cleaning.

- **Documents and art** tell us that there were female priests until the New Kingdom. Many served as priestesses of the goddess Hathor.

- **Ordinary Egyptians were not allowed** inside the inner regions of the temples, and only saw the temple images of the gods during festival processions. They left offerings to the gods in the outer temple courts.

- **Priests were paid** with the offerings in the temple. The essence of these were thought to be consumed by the gods, but the priests ate the physical substance. Most priests worked in a shift system.

- **Some priests had specialist skills** and knowledge. In some parts of Egypt 'hour priests' skilled in astronomy were charged with determining when key festivals took place.

- **Priests had to wash** twice during the day and twice during the night. They also had to be clean-shaven, without body hair, and circumcised. They were not allowed to wear wool or leather.

- **Although religious knowledge** was not a necessary requirement for entering the priesthood, there were strict rules governing the profession.

- **Priests were forbidden** to discuss what went on inside a temple.

▼ The mortuary temple of Queen Hatshepsut. Inside, 163 mummies of high-priests have been discovered.

Temples

- **A temple was a building** or buildings that was considered to be the house of a god.

- **The most important part** of any temple was the shrine, where the statue of the god was kept.

- **Each temple was dedicated** to a god, or family of gods. Priests and priestesses served the statue with food and played music to it.

- **Few pre-New Kingdom temples** have survived as they were built of reeds or mud-brick.

- **Egyptian temples were not public.** They were usually visited only by priests and king.

- **Large temples** were funded by the state. Some became small towns, with villages for priests and workers.

- **Temples were used as grain banks.** Taxes of grain were collected, and then redistributed to workers as wages.

- **From the Middle Kingdom onwards**, massive gateways called pylons were added to the temples.

- **These pylons were often flanked** by two monuments called obelisks.

- **The Egyptians held many festivals** to celebrate their gods.

◀ *Massive pylons often flanked the entrance to great Egyptian temples such as Luxor, followed by a large courtyard.*

Life after death

- **The ancient Egyptians** believed that if you prayed to the gods and mummified the body, it was possible to live on after death.

- **They believed** that parts of a person lived on after death – the soul ('Akh'), the life force ('Ka'), and the memory and personality ('Ba').

- **After death**, the body was mummified. Then the Ka was reactivated for the transformation of rebirth.

- **The Ka had to journey** through the underworld of Duat, believed to exist below the Earth.

- **The Books of the Dead** were decorated scrolls of papyrus made as passports through Duat.

- **Before entering the afterlife**, the deceased had to deny all the evil they might done in their lifetime.

- **A dead person's heart** was weighed against Maat. The scales were held by Anubis.

- **If you passed this test**, you were fit to enter paradise.

- **If you failed the test**, your heart was devoured by a beast. You would not survive the afterlife.

- **If you failed to enter paradise**, you were sent back as a spirit to the land of the living to be hated and feared.

▼ *After death, the Ba left the body and began the journey from the tomb to the underworld.*

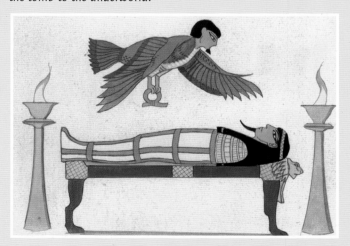

Making a mummy

- **A mummy is a dead body** preserved by drying.

- **The practice of mummification became common** during the Middle Kingdom.

- **It was believed** that by preserving the body, the spirit of the deceased would be able to live again.

- **We know about the process** of mummification from tomb illustrations and from the writings of the Greek historian Herodotus.

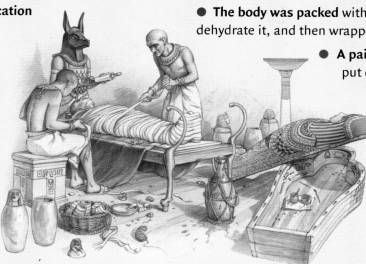

- **The dead body** was washed, and the brain was pulled out through the nose with an iron hook.

- **A slit was made** in the side of the body and the liver, lungs, stomach and intestines were removed and put in canopic jars. The heart was left in place.

- **The body was packed** with a chemical called natron to dehydrate it, and then wrapped in bandages.

- **A painted mask** was sometimes put over the mummy's head. In the case of a king this was ornate.

- **The mummy** was then placed in the coffin, ready for the funeral.

◄ *The priest in charge of mummification represented the god Anubis.*

Funerals and burials

- **Poor Egyptians** were buried in shallow round pits with a few of their possessions.

- **Wealthy Egyptian** were taken to their resting place in a funerary cortege with priests, family members and even a group of professional mourners.

- **The family** walked behind the coffin. As a sign of respect, men were unshaven.

- **Offerings were made** in the name of the pharaoh, as he was the connection between men and the gods.

- **At the final resting place,** the 'Opening of the Mouth' ritual was performed, to restore the mummy's senses.

- **In the Offering Ritual,** the priest recited spells to ensure the the deceased had all it needed in the afterlife.

- **By the time of the Old Kingdom**, the rich were buried in grand tombs called *mastabas*.

- **Mastabas contained chapels** with false doors. The Egyptians believed that the spirit of the deceased receive offerings through them and then return to the afterlife.

- **The soul of the dead** was believed to journey with the sun around the world.

- **By the late New Kingdom**, and with the threat of tomb robberies, the lavish tombs were replaced with secretive burials in places that could be more easily protected.

◄ *In 'the opening of the mouth', the jaw of the coffin was 'opened' using an adze (a tool with a bronze blade). This wall painting shows Ay performing the ceremony for Tutankhamun.*

A king's resting place

- **Pyramids have square bases** and four triangular sides sloping up to the top to a pointed tip.

- **Egypt's pyramids** are on the west bank of the Nile.

- **The stepped pyramid** contained a series of burial chambers for the king and his family.

- **The stepped pyramid** was surrounded by a series of courtyards in which festivals were held.

- **The contents of the stepped pyramid** at Saqqara were looted long ago. When archaeologists entered the tomb, only a mummified foot remained!

- **Pharaoh Sneferu built the first smooth pyramid.** It was built from slabs and the steps were filled in.

- **Three great pyramids** were built at Giza, for the pharaohs Menkaura, Khafra and Khufu.

- **The largest pyramid** is the Great Pyramid of Khufu at Giza. It was built for Pharaoh Khufu around 2550 BC.

- **Ten pyramids** stand at Giza. Three pharaohs insisted that pyramids for their wives be built alongside their own.

- **The architecture of the pyramids** has influenced architects around the world.

▼ The complex at Giza contains Khufu's Great Pyramid, and the pyramids of Khafra and Menkaura.

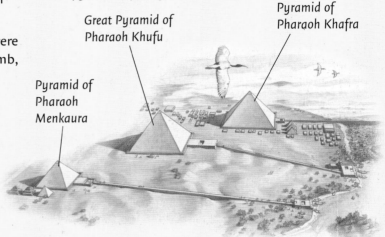

Great Pyramid of Pharaoh Khufu

Pyramid of Pharaoh Khafra

Pyramid of Pharaoh Menkaura

The Great Pyramid

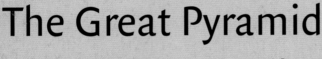

- **The Great Pyramid** of Giza was constructed for Pharaoh Khufu about 4500 years ago.

- **The sides of the pyramid** were covered with white limestone, and the tip was capped with gold.

- **Inside the Great Pyramid,** a labyrinth of passages lead to the king's chamber.

- **An investigation** of air shafts leading from the queen's chamber in 1993 revealed a blockage, which might be a fourth chamber.

- **The Great Pyramid was emptied** by robbers, but archaeologists did find a coffin inside the king's chamber.

- **The Great Pyramid contains** about 2 million blocks of stone, each weighing over 2 tons.

- **On the east side of the Great Pyramid** stands Khufu's mortuary temple and in front stands the Sphinx.

◄ The Egyptians believed that the sculpture of the Sphinx had magical powers that would help protect the tombs and temples it watched over.

- **The Sphinx was a mythical beast**, with the body of a lion and the head of a king.

- **In the 19th century,** tourists paid to be carried up to the top of Khufu's pyramid. Many were killed on the treacherous climb, and it is now against the law.

- **Today, the modern Egyptian capital, Cairo,** is not far from the Great Pyramid. The stone is being damaged by pollution from the cars and factories of the busy city.

Valley of the Queens

- **The Valley of the Queens**, at Thebes, was the main cemetery for royal wives and children during the New Kingdom.

- **There are about 75 tombs** in the valley.

- **The tombs** of the Valley of the Queens were discovered by the Italian archaeologist Ernesto Schiaparelli at the start of the 20th century.

- **The most famous** tomb belongs to Queen Nefertari, wife of Ramesses II (1279–1213 BC).

◀ The tomb of Nefertari has the best preserved paintings of any Egyptian site yet discovered.

- **Nefertari's tomb** contains art depicting the queen worshipping Osiris and offering milk to the goddess Hathor.

- **Despite the Valley's name**, it also contains the tombs of several princes of the New Kingdom.

- **Prince Kamuast** had a brightly decorated tomb similar to that of a pharaoh, but much smaller.

- **Scenes in Prince Khaemweset's tomb** show him being presented to the guardians of the gates with his father.

- **Thiti is thought to be the wife** of Ramesses IV. Her tomb has now been restored.

> ★ **STAR FACT** ★
> The Valley of the Queens was once known as Ta-Set-Neferu ('the place of the Children of the Pharaoh').

Valley of the Kings

- **The Valley of the Kings** lies on the west bank of the Nile.

- **The eastern valley** is the burial place of kings of the 18th–20th Dynasties. The western valley contains four tombs, including that of Amenhotep III.

- **At first, tomb entrances** were disguised. When this practice ended, guards were appointed to watch over the tombs instead.

- **Most tombs** were cut into the limestone, and contained corridors, an antechamber and a sarcophagus chamber.

- **The corridors ended with the burial chamber** where the pharaoh's body was placed.

- **The Valley required the skills** of dozens of workmen who lived in the village of Deir-el-Medina.

- **The tomb of Seti I** is the longest in the valley and is covered with colourful paintings.

- **Tutankhamun's tomb** is one of the smallest.

- **Despite all precautions,** nearly all the tombs in the Valley of the Kings have been looted.

- **Legend says** the Valley of the Kings was protected by the goddess Meretseger.

▶ Tutankhamun's tomb contains a burial chamber and a treasury.

Magic and ritual

◀ The scarab amulet is made in the form of a scarab beetle. It was the symbol of Khepri, the sun god associated with resurrection, and was one of the most common types of amulets worn.

● **The ancient Egyptians** believed that magical powers came from the gods. The source of these powers was a force called *heka*, used to create the world and protect it from the forces of chaos.

● **They also believed** the gods bestowed magical powers on the pharaohs. Priests and magicians were also thought to possess magical powers.

● **Hundreds of books** containing magic spells were kept in temple libraries. Some priests specialized in magic.

● **Many Egyptians thought** that magic could be used to manipulate people's behaviour. It was believed that a magician could use war spells to defend a country from invaders.

● **Some days** were regarded as unlucky in ancient Egypt. Papyrus calendars have some days ringed in red, a colour thought to represent the dry desert, and thus bad fortune.

● **For a magic spell to be successful**, the Egyptians believed that it had to be performed when the conditions were perfect. Dusk and dawn were thought to be good times to cast spells. It was also important that the ingredients for the spell were pure and of good quality.

● **Spells were often accompanied** by a ritual. Some spells required the magician to just wave their hands, while in other spells miniature figurines had to be burned, spat upon or stabbed for the spell to work.

● **Archaeologists have found special bricks** embedded in the side of several New Kingdom tombs. These were sets of four mud-bricks that the Egyptians believed were magical, and would protect the deceased from evil.

● **Each magic brick** held a specific object – an amulet, an Anubis or a shabti figure. Text from the *Book of the Dead* was inscribed on the bricks to defend the deceased from the enemies of Osiris.

▲ The city of Mendes was the centre of the cult of the goddess Hat-Mehit, who was known as chief of the fishes. For this reason, fish amulets were commonly worn here.

▲ The eye of Horus represented the act of healing. Amulets of this symbol were worn for protection and strength.

★ STAR FACT ★
Magic wands were made of bronze or ivory. Sometimes they were shaped like snakes because the goddess of magic, Selket, was depicted as a snake.

Saqqara

▶ Many of the tombs at Saqqara contain spectacular wall paintings.

● **Saqqara was part of the royal cemetery** of Memphis.

● **It was in use as a burial ground** from the 1st Dynasty to the Christian period.

● **The step pyramid of Djoser**, built around 2650 BC, had an underground burial chamber lined with granite, and a sealed chamber.

● **Saqqara was the resting place** for many generations of pharaohs.

● **The Pyramid Texts** were a series of beautiful spells carved into the walls of some of the pyramids at Saqqara.

● **During the New Kingdom**, many important officials moved to Memphis. When they died, they were buried at Saqqara.

● **By the Late Period**, many sacred animals were being buried at the north end of Saqqara. These included baboons, ibis and hawks.

● **Most of the tombs at Saqqara** were built of very small stone blocks.

● **By the time of the Greek-Roman period**, Saqqara had become a centre for pilgrims, but it remained a burial place for Egyptian leaders until the arrival of Christianity.

Dreams

● **The ancient Egyptians believed** that dreams held great power and called them 'revelations of the truth'. They were seen as a way of communicating the will of the gods and predicting the future.

● **The library of Scribe Kenherkhopeshef** contained a Dream Book papyrus. It contains the interpretations of over 100 dreams.

● **Dream interpretation** was often based on a verbal connection. The Egyptian words for 'donkey' and 'great' were the same, so a dream about a donkey meant good luck.

● **Thutmose IV was told in a dream** that if he cleared away the sand from the feet of the Sphinx at Giza he would become king of Egypt.

● **Revelatory dreams** were thought to be very important. These were dreams that might show the dreamer the location of hidden treasure or a medicine to cure a sick patient.

★ STAR FACT ★

Dream Books have been found dating back to the Old Kingdom. They list dreams such as breaking stones, losing teeth, having one's face turn into a leopard, drinking warm beer and drowning in the Nile.

● **'Teachings for Merikare'**, written by King Kheti between 2070 and 2100 BC, took the opposite approach. It advised that dreams actually meant the opposite of what they appeared to be about.

● **It was also believed** that dreams allowed the living to see the activities of the deceased.

● **From the Late Period**, people began to sleep in temple complexes hoping that the intentions of the gods might be communicated to them through divinely inspired dreams.

● **Special priests** were appointed from the Late Period onward to interpret these dreams. These priests were known by the Greek term 'onirocrites'.

Houses and gardens

- **According to the Greek historian** Diodorus Siculus, Egyptian dwellings were constructed of papyrus reeds until the 1st century BC.

- **More sophisticated houses** were built using sun-dried bricks

- **The rooms of larger houses** were arranged around a courtyard or on either side of a corridor.

- **A worker's house** had between two and four rooms, and an enclosed courtyard.

- **The houses of the rich** had several bedrooms, reception rooms and private quarters.

▶ Noblemen usually had large houses in extensive grounds, surrounded by high walls.

- **Water was drawn from wells** from the time of the New Kingdom. The water was raised with a shaduf into a pond.

- **Town houses** stood two to three storeys high. Many people slept on their flat roofs in summer.

- **Gardens were popular**. Egyptian art shows gardens ranging from a few fruit trees to great botanical gardens.

- **Egyptian art** suggest that gardens may have been very formal.

- **Gardeners were often employed** by wealthy Egyptians and in temples.

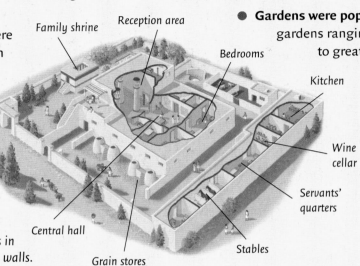

Family shrine · Reception area · Bedrooms · Kitchen · Wine cellar · Servants' quarters · Stables · Grain stores · Central hall

Hunting

- **The first people** in Egypt hunted wild animals, including ostriches, gazelles and giraffes.

- **Birds provided a rich source of food**, and were hunted and killed by hurling wooden throwsticks.

- **Small birds** were caught in nets. Large numbers of migrating species were caught when they landed after crossing the Mediterranean.

- **Many examples of Egyptian wall art** depict birds being caught in nets.

- **Fish were caught** in baskets or nets, or were tackled with spears.

- **One species of catfish** had poisonous spines. An Egyptian relief shows a man pulling one of these fish out of the catch and extracting the spine.

★ STAR FACT ★
On a hunting expedition, the pharaoh rode out in his chariot accompanied by soldiers wearing full military dress.

- **Wealthy Egyptians** may have been among the first people to have hunted for pleasure. They chased animals such as antelopes and hares for sport.

- **Egyptian hunting scenes** often show kings tracking wild beasts inside enclosed grounds guarded by soldiers.

- **Hippos were hunted** because they damaged crops.

◀ Hippo hunting was very important – if a king managed to kill a hippo, it was thought to symbolize the slaying of evil.

Creation myths

- **Like many ancient cultures**, the Egyptians' creation stories tried to explain how life began.

- **One creation myth** suggested that the world had been made by a god called Ptah by the power of thought.

- **Another story** puts forward the idea that the universe was originally a sea of chaos inside a god called Nun.

- **Nun was a god of chaos** and infinity, greatly feared by the ancient Egyptians. They believed that he might one day sink the world back into the ocean of chaos.

- **They also believed** that Nun was responsible for darkness.

- **Ra was the god of the sun** and light. The Egyptians believed that a blue lotus flower appeared on the dark waters of Nun, and unfurled its petals to reveal Ra, who then created the world.

◀ *The Sun is linked with many of the Egyptian creation myths.*

- **The Egyptians believed** the sun was rolled across the sky every day by the god Khepri.

- **Night and day** was explained by the story of the twin gods Nut and Keb. They hugged each other so tightly they blocked out the sun's rays.

- **To create daylight**, Ra ordered that the twins be separated and Nut was raised up to become the sky. Keb became the Earth. As night fell, the twins were reunited, as Nut came down to earth to be with her brother.

- **The Egyptians believed** that the sun god Ra was the first pharaoh.

Dance

▶ *Dancing was often combined with gymnastics and acrobatics.*

- **The ancient Egyptians loved to dance**. Pottery vessels dating from before the Pre-Dynastic period have been found, decorated with dancers.

- **Professional dancers** were usually women. Scenes suggest they wore skirts or loose tunics with shoulder straps.

- **Many ancient wall paintings and carvings** depict scenes of Egyptians singing and dancing.

- **Dancers also performed acrobatics** including backbends, flips, cartwheels, high-kicks and handstands.

- **Archaeologists have yet to find** any depictions of men and women dancing together. The most common scenes show solo dancers, or groups of female dancers.

- **During the Old Kingdom**, funerals often included dance. Dance was an expression of mourning for the dead.

- **The *mww*-dancers performed** as the funeral procession reached the tomb. Their dance symbolized the dead being led to the underworld.

- **Dance was a way of celebrating** the joy and revelry of feast days.

- **Dancing in temples** marked important festivals such as the jubilee (Sed) ceremony.

- **Dancing dwarfs** were a special attraction. The Egyptians believed that they never grew old because they never grew past the height of a child.

Music

- **Egyptian art suggests** that musicians were nearly always men in the Old Kingdom. By the time of the New Kingdom, they were mostly women.

- **There is no evidence** to suggest that the ancient Egyptians used any form of musical notation.

- **Rhythms were beaten out** on tambourines, drums, cymbals and bells.

▼ *Stringed instruments such as harps and lutes were often played during banquets in ancient Egypt.*

- **Stringed instruments** included the lyre (a form of lute) and the harp.

- **Wind instruments** included wooden pipes and early flutes. Bugle-like trumpets were used in religious ceremonies and in battle.

- **Festivals and holy days** were marked by music and singing.

- **Such festivals were frequent.** One village in the Fayum region dedicated 150 days every year to festivals.

- **Music was also** a part of everyday life, providing a natural rhythm to workers' tasks.

- **In Old and Middle Kingdom tombs**, inscriptions of songs and hymns were sung to the accompaniment of a harp to celebrate the dead.

- **Both men and wome**n could be musicians in ancient Egypt, but there were some instruments that were played only by men, and some that were played only by women.

Sports

- **It was important** that young men were in good physical condition because it was always possible that they would have to go into the army.

- **A wide variety of sports were played,** from wrestling and weightlifting, to a host of ball games.

- **The ancient Egyptians invented** many aspects of sport still in use today, including neutral referees and uniforms for players.

- **The sport of handball** was played by four women. Each had to throw the ball to the other at the same time.

- **The Saqqara tombs** depict boxing scenes. Pharaohs and princes paid to watch.

◄ *Scenes of ancient Egyptians boxing for sport were found in the tomb of 'Mery Ra' and the 'Ptah Hotep' tomb in Saqqara.*

- **Balls made of leather skins** filled with reeds were used in a number of hockey-type games.

- **Swimming was the most popular** competitive sport. People practised in the Nile.

- **Running** was an important sport. It had a religious significance when a new pharaoh was being crowned.

- **As part of the coronation**, the pharaoh ran around a temple before spectators.

- **Archery was a popular sport**, and the practise of it was also important training for battle.

Games and toys

- **Board games** were popular in ancient Egypt. Games and toys are among the oldest items found in Egypt.

- **In the game 'Senet',** the object was to move your pieces from one end to the other.

- **One of the oldest board games** was *Mehen*, or 'snake'. Players moved pieces around a spiral board.

- **The game 'Hounds and Jackals'** may be the forerunner of Snakes and Ladders. The oldest board found dates from the First Intermediate Period.

- **Toys were simple** and were made of wood, stone, ivory, ceramics or bone.

- **The British Museum** holds a model of a crocodile with a moving jaw. Toys with moving parts have been found at el Lisht.

- **Children played against each other** for marbles.

★ **STAR FACT** ★
Archaeologists have discovered mysterious rows of holes bored into the roofs and floors of Egyptian temples. Some think that these were used for a board game called Wari, which is still played in Africa today.

- **Egyptian children played** games such as leapfrog, tug-of-war, arm-wrestling and juggling.

- **Many of the games** Egyptian children played may have been early versions of modern games such as Grandmother's Footsteps and Blind-man's Buff.

◀ *Board games were a popular family pursuit. Children played with simple toys that were often home-made.*

Ancient storytelling

- **Egyptian stories** were passed on verbally through generations.

- **Stories were told for entertainment** but many also contained moral messages.

- **The earliest written story** dates from the Middle Kingdom.

- **Ancient autobiographies** have been discovered, such as the life story of the official Weni, who served from the reign of King Teti to that of King Merenre.

- **One of the oldest stories** was the tale of the courtier Sinuhe. It tells of his flight from Egypt after the death of King Amenemhat.

- **After many years,** Sinuhe writes a letter to King Senusret I, who allows him to be reinstated at court.

◀ *The legend of Osiris tells that he was the dead form of an earthly ruler who rose from the dead to become king of the gods.*

- **The tale** *The Book of the Cow of Heaven* described how the sun god Ra sent Hathor to quash a rebellion by mankind.

- **In the story of Setne Khamwas**, a son of Ramesses II encounters the ghost of a dead magician in his tomb.

- **In the** *Tale of the Unlucky Prince,* the Seven Hathors predict that a baby prince will die because he will be attacked by a crocodile, a snake or a dog. The end of the papyrus is missing, so it is not known how the story ends.

- **Travel stories** that featured magic were popular. In *The Tale of the Shipwrecked Sailor,* a sailor is stranded on an island after a storm. A giant serpent rescues him before the island mysteriously sinks beneath the waves.

Zoos, parks and exotic gardens

● **The keeping of animals** for pleasure was common in ancient Egypt. Zoos were popular, and many kept dangerous wild animals.

● **Exotic animals** such as elephants, bears, giraffes and ostriches usually entered Egypt in official trading expeditions, or as tribute (tax) that Nubia and other parts of the empire had to pay to Egypt.

● **The earliest-known captive polar bear** was owned by Ptolemy II at his private zoo at Alexandria.

● **Queen Hatshepsut** was very interested in wild beasts. She kept a number of baboons, which she was given when she had myrrh saplings brought from the Horn of Africa.

● **Pharaoh Akhenaten** kept wild animals and a bird aviary at his northern palace at the city of Akhetaten.

● **Animals were sometimes treated very poorly.** The story *Lion in Search of Man* details a horrific practice given out to a bear whose claws and teeth were removed.

● **The wild animals** that Pharaoh Thutmose III collected can be seen in an engraving of a botanical garden in the festival temple at Karnak. It shows deer, birds, cattle and a number of other animals that were imported from countries such as Syria.

★ **STAR FACT** ★
During the 5th Dynasty, Syrian bears were brought to Egypt. They were kept on leashes in the homes of the wealthy, who seemed to have little regard for their own safety.

● **Ramesses III** developed a great interest in gardens. He ordered a great park to be planted near his father's house, with vines and olive trees 'so that people may sit in the shade.'

● **Public parks** were occasionally vandalized. The scribe Petosiris (300 BC) recorded: 'This place, the wretches trampled it. Anyone walked through it. They ate the fruit of its trees, they carried the reeds to the houses of all and sundry.'

▶ *Rich Egyptians kept collections of wild animals which included exotic creatures such as lions, tigers and giraffes.*

Festivals

● **Hundreds of festivals** were celebrated by the people of the kingdom. Calendars on temple walls reveal that some temples marked dozens of religious holidays a year.

● **In the festival hall** of Thutmose III at Karnak, a list details the 54 feast days that were celebrated every year.

● **Many of these festivals** involved carrying an image of the god from one temple to another. This allowed ordinary Egyptians a glimpse of the image.

● **The Festival of Opet** was celebrated from the early 18th Dynasty onwards in the second month of the season of the *akhet* (flood) season.

● **The Festival of the Valley** took place at Thebes from the 18th Dynasty onwards. The statues of Amun, Mut and Khons were carried from Karnak to Deir El-Bahri.

● **The festival of the fertility god Min** was celebrated during the first month of the *shemu* (harvesting) season. The statue of the god was carried out of its temple and placed on a platform in the country.

★ **STAR FACT** ★
Divine images were usually carried by priests in special gilded boats that were fixed to the top of poles.

● **A festival was held** to mark the murder of Osiris. His tragic story was performed, and the whole country went into mourning. After several days, priests announced that he had risen from the dead, and only then were people allowed to celebrate.

● **On festival days**, temple altars were piled high with food and drink. For the poor, these events represented a rare opportunity to taste delicacies such as wine and roast beef.

● **A huge quantity of food** was consumed during festivals. During the Opet festival more than 11,000 loaves and cakes were eaten, and 385 measures of beer were consumed. At the Sokar festival, more than 7400 loaves were eaten and nearly 1500 measures of beer were drunk.

Scribes

● **The term scribe** is a translation of the Egyptian word *sesh*, meaning the government administrators of the Egyptian kingdom. Scribes were civil servants.

◄ *Writing materials used by scribes included papyrus, reed pens, and pots that were used to hold ink.*

● **Scribes wrote diplomatic letters,** calculated taxes, took notes during court cases and organized building projects.

● **Positions as scribes** were highly coveted and the profession became hereditary.

● **The scribe** was often depicted with legs crossed, and his papyrus across his lap.

● **Thoth was the god of scribes**. He was shown as a man with the head of an ibis bird, carrying a pen and scrolls.

● **The profession of scribe** was considered privileged.

● **Evidence of a school for scribes** has been found at Deir el-Medina.

● **A scribe's kit** consisted of a palette with two holes in it, into which cakes of ink could be inserted. There was space for reed pens, a water pot, and a knife for trimming papyrus. A stone was carried to smooth the paper.

● **One of Egypt's most famous scribes** was Ahmas (1680–1620 BC). One of his best-known writings was the text 'Accurate reckoning, the entrance into the knowledge of all existing things and all obscure secrets'.

● **The scribe Imhotep** lived 4500 years ago. He was a high priest and also designed the world's first pyramid at Saqqara. After his death, the ancient Egyptians came to see him as a god.

Hieroglyphics

▶ Hieroglyphs were painted or carved into walls. Many are still visible in tombs.

● **Hieroglyphics is a form** of writing using symbols. There were about 700 symbols in the system.

● **The word 'hieroglyph' is Greek,** meaning 'sacred carving'.

● **Hieroglyphics was often written** on a form of paper called papyrus. It was named after the plant from which it was made.

● **Hieroglyph symbol images** were usually pictures from the natural world of Egypt. The letter 'M', for example, was represented by the barn owl.

● **Some hieroglyphs represent sounds**, others stand for ideas.

● **Hieroglyphics could be written** from left to right, right to left or from top to bottom.

● **Hieratic was a simplified form** of hieroglyphics. This script was used for business transactions and religious documents.

● **In the first millennium** BC a script called *demotic* began to replace hieratic. This was followed in the 1st century BC by a form called Coptic Script.

● **Coptic Script** contained the 24 letters of the Greek alphabet and six signs from the demotic script.

● **By the 6th century** AD, when the last Egyptian temple was closed after the fall of the Roman Empire, the art of reading hieroglyphs was lost until 1799.

Art

● **The first pieces of Egyptian art** were scratched onto cave walls around 5000 BC.

● **Artists were often commissioned** to paint pictures of important Egyptians after they had died.

● **Artists learned their craft** when they were young. At first they were given tasks such as mixing colours and fetching wate.

● **Different minerals were used to make different colours** – carbon for black, ochre for red and yellow, and azurite and malachite for green and blue.

● **Teams of master artists** worked on large wall paintings.

● **In Egyptian art**, figures are not usually depicted face on. A person's head is usually turned right or left. The eye is always shown in full frontal view.

▶ Egyptian artists painted pharaohs, food and other items that the deceased might need in the afterlife on tomb walls.

● **As a result,** paintings of figures were not realistic, as a single portrait included a variety of viewpoints.

● **Paintings were usually hierarchal in scale**. A king would be shown much larger than his servants, who were ranked in size according to their importance.

● **Some of the best-preserved paintings** are murals in the rooms that lead to tombs.

● **Draughtsmen were called** *sesh kedut* – 'writers of outlines'.

Mathematics

● **The Greeks are usually credited** with inventing mathematics. However, the oldest recorded evidence for the use of mathematics was found in ancient Egypt and dated back to around 2000 BC.

● **Reading and writing numbers** in ancient Egypt was relatively simple. It used a system of symbols. The higher number was always written in front of the lower number.

● **There was no sign for zero** in the Egyptian numerical system. Scribes sometimes left a gap between numbers where a zero should be.

● **The Egyptian decimal system** used seven symbols.

● **The ancient Egyptians** had no abstract formulae like the Greeks. Instead, they tackled mathematical problems by a series of smaller calculations.

● **Our knowledge of Egyptian mathematics** is based on a tiny number of texts. The only evidence found so far comes from four papyri, a leather scroll and two wooden tablets.

● **The Rhind Mathematical Papyrus**, found in a tomb in Thebes, is packed full of fractions and complex calculations relating to the volumes of triangles, rectangles and pyramids.

● **The Egyptians used mathematics** in calculating how to set out the great pyramids. By working out the area of a circle according to the length of its diameter they could calculate the volume of a pyramid.

● **Scribes learned mathematics** by copying set examples and replacing figures with their own answers. Archaeologists have discovered ancient exercise sheets, with teacher's markings on them.

Craftwork

▶ *Craftworkers were responsible for designing the great buildings and monuments of the Pharaonic era.*

● **The ancient Egyptians** were skilful carpenters.

● **Very little timber** was readily available in Egypt. Apart from a few acacia trees, tamarisk and willow, most of the wood was imported from Lebanon.

● **An adze** was used for carving and planing. It had a wooden handle and a blade.

● **Early forms of drills** were rotated by an implement like an archer's bow.

● **The tomb of Rekhmire at Thebes** contains a series of pictures of carpenters, which reveal the many tools they used.

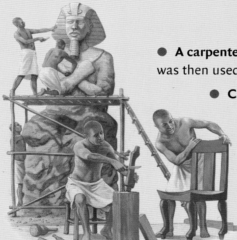

● **A carpenter worked on rough wood** with an axe. A saw was then used to slice into the wood.

● **Carpenters used a vice** to hold pieces of wood when sawing. The piece of timber was tied to a pole that was rammed into the ground.

● **Bones were ground** to make glue. Gesso was made by mixing whiting with glue. It was harder than plaster, stuck better to wood and was a good base for painting.

● **Stones were used** to scour wood to ensure there were no rough edges.

Making fine things

▶ Most gold arrived in Egypt from Nubia. It was weighed and then sent to workshops.

● **Egyptian jewellers** used gold, silver and semi-precious stones.

● **By the Middle Kingdom,** gold was the most precious material in Egypt.

● **The process of casting** was used to make many metal objects. Metal was heated until it became liquid and then poured into moulds.

● **Gold was mined** from the Eastern Desert and from Nubia, where Egyptian inscriptions date back to 3100 BC.

● **The technique of welding** was used by jewellers from the Middle Kingdom onwards.

● **In welding, different metals were heated,** then the whole artefact was joined over a furnace and a blowpipe was used to increase the heat until the two pieces were welded together.

● **The technique of soldering** was in use from the 4th Dynasty onwards.

● **The best example** of the goldsmiths' art are the funeral masks of pharaohs.

● **The first glass beads** were made in Pre-Dynastic times. The first glass vessels were made in the reign of Tuthmosis I in the New Kingdom.

● **Most pottery** was made from red-brown clay, and is called Nile siltware. It was not highly valued.

Around the home

● **Egyptian houses** were furnished simply.

● **Chairs made for use in the home** were made of carved wood. They were covered with leather or cloth and were much lower than modern chairs.

● **Low stools** were used in most homes. By the time of the Middle Kingdom, folding stools were in use.

● **Most Egyptian families** did not have much in the way of spare possessions, but baskets were used to store items when they were not in use.

● **Dining and gaming tables** were round, and mostly made of wood, though some stone and metal tables have been discovered.

● **In wealthier households**, boxes made from wood or ivory replaced baskets.

● **Jewellery and other valuables** were kept in storage chests, which were often highly decorated.

◀ Representations of the god Bes were kept in many homes because he was linked with protection of the family.

● **Drawers were rare in ancient Egypt**, but they were sometimes built into certain pieces of furniture.

● **Lamps were used** in the long winter evenings. Made out of pottery, they were filled with oils such as kiki oil and olive oil, and had floating wicks.

● **Wealthy Eygptians had limestone toilets**. Poorer families made do with toilet stools, under which stood a ceramic bowl.

★ STAR FACT ★
Beds with wooden frames have been traced back to the early dynastic period.

Astronomy and astrology

● **The ancient Egyptians** divided the night sky into 36 groups of star gods or constellations called decons. The most important decon to the Egyptians was the dog star Sirius, which they believed that was the goddess Sopdet.

● **From the Old Kingdom onwards,** the Egyptians believed that humans could be reborn in the form of stars.

● **In ancient writings** called the Pyramid Texts, the author asks for the sky goddess Nut to place him 'among the imperishable stars.'

● **Astronomy was used** to predict the changes of the seasons. The Egyptians noted the times when Sirius rose with the Sun. This was called the 'Sothic rising', and it indicated that the flood season would soon arrive.

● **The ceremony of Pedj Shes** (Stretching the Cord) dates back to 2686 BC. It was performed to determine the correct alignment for the building of foundations of the pyramids. It relied on sightings of Orion and the Great Bear constellations.

● **The 'Sothic rising' of Sirius** coincided with the beginning of the solar year (the number of days it takes for the Earth to orbit the Sun) once every 1460–1456 years. The time between these risings is called the 'Sothic Cycle'.

● **The earliest evidence of true astronomical knowledge** in Egypt are diagonal calendars, found painted on the coffin lids of early Middle Kingdom and Late Period.

● **By the Middle Kingdom** the Egyptians had identified five of the planets: Jupiter, Mars, Mercury, Saturn and Venus. They believed the planets were gods.

● **The first appearance of the zodiac** we know today was during the Ptolemaic period. It was painted on the ceiling of the chapel of Osiris on the roof of the temple of Hathor at Dendera in the 1st century AD.

> ★ **STAR FACT** ★
> The Egyptian year was approximately six hours short, so every 40 years, 10 days went missing!

Early travellers

● **Around 450 BC,** the Greek historian Herodotus visited Egypt and recorded the beliefs of its people.

● **In the 1st century AD,** a Greek priest and philosopher called Plutarch studied religious beliefs in Egypt.

● **In 1589 a merchant,** referred to as the Anonymous Venetian, penned an account of a journey to Upper Egypt.

● **The first accurate measurements** of the pyramids were taken in 1638 by an English astronomer called John Graves. He visited Giza and wrote *Pyrmaidographia*.

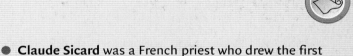

◀ *The French leader Napoleon Bonaparte was amazed by the pyramids, declaring, "From atop these pyramids, forty centuries look down upon you."*

● **Claude Sicard** was a French priest who drew the first accurate map of Egypt. It showed the major monuments, and ancient cities.

● **English traveller James Bruce** discovered the tomb of Ramesses III in the Valley of the Kings in 1768.

● **In 1798 Napoleon Bonaparte invaded Egypt,** taking with him 40 scientists.

● **The scientists' findings** were published in 1809 in a book called *Description de l'Egypte*.

● **Auguste Mariette** was a French archaeologist who discovered the catacomb of the sacred Apis bulls at Saqqara, and the Valley Temple of the pyramid of Chephren at Giza.

● **British Egyptologist William Flinders Petrie** arrived in Egypt in 1880. His important excavations included the Pre-Dynastic necropolis of Naqada.

David Roberts

- **David Roberts (1796–1864) was born** near Edinburgh, Scotland.

- **He first worked** for a travelling circus painting scenary, but his true skills lay as an illustrator.

- **Roberts began to establish a reputation,** and forged friendships with creative minds of the day, including Charles Dickens and the artist J M W Turner.

- **The artist started to attract** patrons such as Lord Northwick, for whom he completed the *Departure of the Israelites* in 1829.

- **At this point** Roberts had never visited the Middle East, and he worked from detailed descriptions and sketches.

- **In 1838, Roberts had enough money** to tour the monuments of ancient Egypt. He travelled by boat to Cairo, where he sketched the pyramids and Sphinx.

- **Roberts' journey** took him as far as Abu Simbel. On the journey he sketched the monuments and landscape.

- **Belgian engraver Louis Haghe** produced 247 lithographs from Roberts' drawings.

- **In 1839 he travelled** from Cairo through Suez, Sinai and Petra, and into modern-day Lebanon.

- **Roberts described the Nile** as 'wending its way like a long winding sheet spangled with silver tears.'

▼ *David Roberts' sketches gave many people their first glimpse of the pyramids and the Sphinx.*

William Flinders Petrie

- **William Flinders Petrie** was taught the art of map-making by his father.

- **By the age of 22** Petrie had written a book on ancient measurements used in prehistoric Britain.

- **Petrie's interest in Egypt** was fostered by books written by Charles Piazzi-Smyth on the Great Pyramid of Giza.

- **Petrie went to Egypt** between 1880 and 1882 to test the mathematical measurements in Piazzi-Smyth's book.

- **Petrie discovered** that every measurement Piazzi-Smyth had taken was inaccurate. His own survey, the *Pyramids and Temples of Giza*, was published in 1883.

- **Petrie established** what later became the British School of Archaeology in Egypt.

- **He was also appointed** the first Edwards Professor of Egyptology at University College in London, holding the post between 1892 and 1933.

- **Petrie discovered** a long period of civilization before the 1st Dynasty – the Pre-Dynastic Period.

- **Petrie was supported financially** by the writer Amelia Edwards. She was the founder of the Egypt Exploration Fund.

- **Petrie earned the Arabic nickname** 'Abu Bagousheh' – father of pots. On every trip to Egypt, he brought back heavily notated samples of pottery.

◄ *Petrie's book, The Pyramids and Temples of Giza, is still a respected piece of work today.*

Carter's discovery

● **One of the most dramatic** archaeological discoveries of all time was made in November 1922, when the English archaeologist Howard Carter discovered the virtually untouched tomb of the pharaoh Tutankhamun.

● **Carter was born in England** in 1874, and worked as an assistant to the archaeologist William Flinders Petrie. He was offered the job of Inspector of General of Monuments in Upper Egypt, based in Luxor, in 1899.

● **In 1905, Carter resigned** from the position. In 1907 he met English aristocrat Lord Carnarvon, who had a passion for archaeology. Carnarvon persuaded Carter to work for him, and Carter carried out a number of excavations on behalf of his employer.

● **Carter and Carnarvon** were granted a licence from the Egyptian Antiquities Service to dig in the Valley of the Kings in 1914. Carter was certain that the tomb of a young pharaoh called Tutankhamun was still buried somewhere in the valley.

● **Carter based his evidence** on a series of archaeological clues. Tutankhamun's name was inscribed on a stela (a carved stone pillar) at the temple of Karnak, and was also found on artefacts found in the Valley of the Kings by the American archaeologist Theodore Davis.

● **World War I delayed work** on the site until 1917. Progress was slow, and by 1921 very little had been found. Lord Carnarvon began to grow uneasy about the amount of money that the project was costing.

● **Carter was given one more year** to dig, beginning in autumn 1922. On 4 November, workmen found a stone step. This proved to be the first of an underground staircase.

● **Excavation work began** on the site. The stairway was cleared, revealing a door, then a second, inner door, which had the name of a pharaoh on it – Tutankhamun.

● **On 26 November**, Carter and his team pierced a hole through the second door. The tomb inside was intact, and was full of some of the most spectacular treasures of ancient Egypt.

● **Emptying the tomb** took nearly a decade. About 3500 items were slowly catalogued and removed, including the fantastic coffin and mummy of the pharaoh.

◀ Carter and one of his team unbrick a wall leading into a passageway and eventually Tutankhamun's treasury. What they found inside remains probably the most spectacular discovery in archaeological history.

The Rosetta Stone

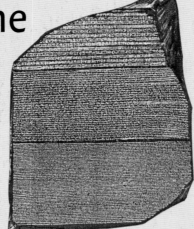

- **The Rosetta Stone** is a piece of granite rock covered with ancient writing.

- **The stela was inscribed** in 196 BC with a decree issued at the city of Memphis. It was discovered in a small village in the Delta called Rosetta.

- **The stone's inscription** was written in hieroglyphic, demotic and Greek. Ancient Greek was understood, so it was theoretically possible to decipher the text by comparing the languages.

- **The Rosetta Stone** was found by Napoleon's team of scientists in 1799.

- **When Napoleon** was defeated by the British, the Rosetta Stone was taken to the British Museum. The European experts realized that the names they understood in the Greek script were the same as those enclosed in ovals (cartouches) in the hieroglyphic script.

- ◀ *The Rosetta Stone is engraved with hieroglyphics at the top, followed by demotic script and finally Greek script.*

- **An Egyptologist** called Thomas Young deciphered the demotic text. He was able to decipher the names of Ptolemy and Cleopatra.

- **Hieroglyphic code** was deciphered by a French scholar called Jean Francois Champollion.

- **Champollion published** the book *Lettre a M. Dacier* to announce his discovery to an incredulous world in 1822.

- **We now know** that the Rosetta Stone was written by a group of priests to honour the pharaoh.

> ★ **STAR FACT** ★
> Champollion visited Egypt in 1828. As the first scientist who could read the inscriptions on temples and tomb walls, he was treated with great reverence.

The temples of Abu Simbel

- **The temples of Abu Simbel** lie on the west bank of the Nile, about 530 mi from Cairo.

- **The larger temple** was dedicated to Ramesses II. Outside it stand four giant statues of the king. The smaller temple was built for his wife Nefertari.

- **Abu Simbel was left undisturbed** until the beginning of the 19th century.

- **The temples** were rediscovered by Jean-Louise Burckhardt in 1813.

- **The temples were a popular attraction** in the 19th century, even when covered in sand.

- **The English explorer William Bankes** tried unsuccessfully to enter Nefertari's temple in 1815.

- ◀ *The largest temple at Abu Simbel is dedicated to three gods and Ramesses II, who was himself deified.*

- **A further unsuccessful attempt** to enter the great temple followed in 1816, led by French consul Bernardino Drovetti.

- **Italian Giovanni Belzoni was the first** man to gain entry to the temple.

- **On 1 August 1817** Belzoni cleared the sand blocking the entrance to the main temple, and became the first person to step inside the temple for hundreds of years.

- **The temple was virtually empty,** but the walls were carved with beautiful reliefs illustrating the military campaigns of Ramesses II.

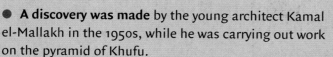

Recent discoveries

- **A discovery was made** by the young architect Kamal el-Mallakh in the 1950s, while he was carrying out work on the pyramid of Khufu.

- **He discovered** the planking of a great ship. It had been dismantled and placed there over 4000 years ago.

- **The Egyptian Antiquities Organization** took 16 years to rebuild the ship.

- **Evidence suggests** that there is another ship buried beside the pyramid of Cheops.

- **An investigation** into the courtyard of Amenophis III in the Luxor temple led to a discovery in 1989.

- **Twenty statues were found** on the western side, mostly dating from the time of Amenophis III.

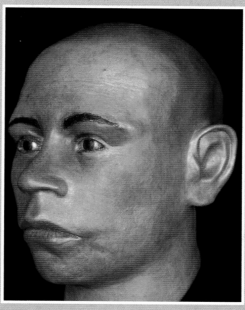

- **Another discovery** was made in 1989 in Akhmim. An 8-m-tall statue of Princess Meritamun was found.

- **In 1989, Michel Redde**, director of the Institut Francais d'Archeologie Orientale of Cairo, found treasure that once belonged to a high priest of the god Serapis.

- **In 1991, archaeologists** discovered the village where the labourers who built the Great Pyramid lived.

- **A Swiss/French mission** in April 2002 discovered a pyramid at the site of Abu Rowash dated to the reign of Djedefre.

◄ *Modern forensic techniques allowed scientists to rebuild the face of pharaoh Tutankhamun, based on his mummy.*

Rescue and salvage archaeology

★ STAR FACT ★
A museum was built at Abu Simbel to house all the finds unearthed during the rebuilding of Abu Simbel.

- **Rescue archaeology** involves carrying out urgent excavations. These occur in areas where developers are waiting to move in, or if environmental changes are threatening a site.

- **In 1959,** the Egyptian government appealed to UNESCO, as the temples of Abu Simbel were in danger of being flooded as a dam was built.

- **Each temple was rebuilt** in a safe location, and an artificial mountain was created.

- **In the modern city** of Alexandria, archaeologist Jean-Yves Empereur is looking for traces of the Tower of Pharos.

- **The remains** of the city of Pharaoh Akhenaten are little more than rubble at present but a project has been launched to reconstruct the central area of the city.

- **In Luxor's Avenue of the Sphinxes**, some of Egypt's treasured structures are turning to dust. A remedy is being investigated.

- **In November 2002**, UNESCO began assessing water damage at Luxor Temple.

- **Plans to construct** a canal across the Sinai Desert would affect archaeological sites. In 1991 a project was launched to suggest a possible alternative route.

- **In 2000**, officials revealed that monuments of the Nile Delta were under threat from building works and rising water levels.

◄ *The Tower of Pharos was built in the Ptolemaic period. Archaeologists have found the foundations.*

Advanced techniques

● **In the past,** mummies have been damaged by archaeologists doing research. Today, scientists use endoscopy instead of conducting an autopsy.

● **X-rays allow scientists** to calculate details such as whether a person suffered any fractures in their lifetime.

● **In 1977,** an international team began fieldwork at Giza, Saqqara and Luxor using geographical techniques such as acoustic sounding.

● **Aerial photography** and thermal infrared imagery techniques have yielded results at Giza, Saqqara and Luxor.

▶ *The mummy of Tutankhamun is prepared for a scan that will reveal its internal structure.*

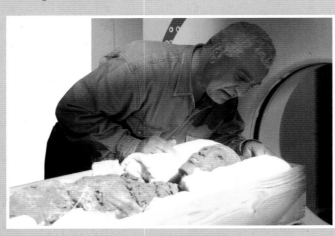

● **A hieroglyphic text** processing programme has been developed in Holland and is now relied upon by Egyptologists around the world.

● **Radar technology** has been used to confirm the existence of a secret chamber in the Great Pyramid of Khufu at Giza.

● **An X-ray** has been carried out on the mummy of Pharaoh Tutankhamun.

● **The pharaoh's mummy** was given a CAT scan to build up a 3-D picture of the bones.

● **The Theban Mapping Project** has created a map and database of every part of Thebes.

● **The project** is also making 3-D computer models of every tomb in Thebes.

Curses and myths

● **Carter was said to have found an inscription** in Tutankhamun's tomb, which read 'Death will slay with his wings whoever disturbs the peace of the pharaoh.'

● **A few months** later, Lord Carnarvon died. The cause of death seemed to be an infection started by an insect bite.

● **When the mummy** of Tutankhamun was unwrapped, it was found to have a wound on the cheek in the same place as the fatal insect bite on Carnarvon.

● **By 1929, eleven people** connected with the discovery of the tomb had died of unnatural causes.

● **Carter's father committed suicide,** leaving a note that read, 'I really cannot stand any more horrors ...so I am making my exit.'

▼ *An inner coffin of Tutankhamun, whose tomb is said to be protected by a potent curse.*

● **Microbiologists have identified** some potentially dangerous spores in ancient tombs.

● **Scientists now wear** protective masks and gloves when unwrapping a mummy.

● **The 5th dynasty Pyramid Texts** contain a tomb curse. It reads: 'As for anyone who shall lay a finger on this pyramid ...he will be one banished, one who eats himself.'

● **A curse has also been found** on the entrance to the tomb of Petety at Giza.

● **A stela belonging to Sarenput I** has a curse inscribed upon it.

DNA and ancient Egypt

- **DNA is a material** in our cells that carries the genetic material for life and determines hereditary characteristics. DNA testing was first developed by scientists in 1985.

- **DNA testing** is now being used to verify the family histories of pharaohs.

- **To extract DNA**, scientists have to take very small samples from body tissue, hair or teeth.

- **In 1994**, Professor Scott Woodward used DNA testing on six Old Kingdom mummies. His tests indicated that two of the mummies had been put in the wrong coffins!

- **Woodward later tested 27 royal mummies** from the New Kingdom period. These samples revealed that Ahmose I had married his sister Seknet-re.

- **The Manchester Museum in England** is the home of the International Mummy Database and Tissue Bank. Here DNA testing techniques are applied to samples of mummies from around the world.

◀ *DNA is the tiny molecule inside every human cell that carries genes in a code. DNA testing can help Egyptologists build a clearer picture of the correct chronology of Egyptian kings.*

- **Dr Moamina Kamal** of Cairo University Medical School has used DNA testing to discover where the workers who built the pyramids came from.

- **In 2000**, a mummy believed to be Ramesses I that had lain in a museum for over 100 years, was DNA tested against Ramesses I's son and grandson.

- **In 2002**, DNA testing of Tutankhamun was cancelled by the Egyptian government.

- **The Egyptian Government** granted permission to harvest DNA from Tutankhamun's eldest child.

Museums around the world

- **Today, there are museums** around the world displaying collections of Egyptian artefacts.

- **The Egyptian Museum in Cairo** was established in 1835. It houses an incredible 120,000 items.

- **The Berlin Egyptian Museum** exhibits include a 3000-year-old portrait bust of Queen Nefertiti.

- **After the construction** of the High Dam at Aswan, a Nubian museum was opened. Among its artefacts are statues of a Meroitic queen and prince.

- **The Gregorian Egyptian Museum** houses monuments and artefacts from Egypt's Imperial age.

- **The collection at the Carnegie Museum of Natural History** in Pittsburgh, United States, includes Egyptian ceramic and stone vessels, tools, and much more.

▶ *The Louvre's Department of Egyptian Antiquities holds thousands of artefacts dating from the Pre-Dynastic era.*

- **The collection of art** at the Metropolitan Museum in New York includes 36,000 items.

- **The Museum of Fine Arts** in Boston, USA, has one of the most important collections of Egyptian artefacts.

- **The Department of Egyptian Antiquities** at the Musee de Louvre in France contains thousands of pieces, including a mummified cat.

- **The British Museum** holds a spectacular collection which spans 5000 years of history.

INDEX

INDEX